D1473083

To Dorothy
Jerusalem, April 72

THE PROPHET MOTIVE
Israel Today and Tomorrow

George Mikes
THE PROPHET MOTIVE
Israel Today and Tomorrow

Illustrated by Jossi Stern

STEIMATZKY'S AGENCY LTD
in association with
 ANDRE DEUTSCH

FIRST PUBLISHED 1969 BY
ANDRE DEUTSCH LIMITED
105 GREAT RUSSELL STREET
LONDON WC1
COPYRIGHT © 1969 BY GEORGE MIKES
ALL RIGHTS RESERVED
PRINTED IN GREAT BRITAIN BY
EBENEZER BAYLIS AND SON LTD
THE TRINITY PRESS
WORCESTER AND LONDON
233 96091 0

This edition published in Israel
by Steimatzky's Agency Ltd
in association with André Deutsch Ltd

To Eva

Contents

CONTENTS

Introduction

'They can't keep all those territories. How can they administrate them?'

'Eshkol is no Ben Gurion.'

'Golda Meir is no Eshkol.'

'Eban is no Dayan.'

'It's not only a question of administration. Those territories aren't *theirs*, don't you see?'

'What about the atrocity stories? My God, that they can even *talk* of atrocities committed by Jews! Do you believe them?' When there was no reply; '*Can* they be true?'

Shreds of conversation, overheard on the plane between Athens and Tel-Aviv. The passengers were mostly Americans, tourists and delegates to the forthcoming Zionist Congress. How different these slightly worried, subdued, half-critical questions and remarks were from the mood of my first arrival here, almost twenty years before. My fellow-passengers now were troubled by doubts; *then* they were overcome by enthusiasm. When we caught sight of the Land of Israel in 1949, everyone crowded to one side of the plane, nearly overturning it; now we all remained seated and threw affectionate but self-conscious glances towards the shores. *Then* they sang the Jewish National Anthem, now someone simply remarked: 'We're nearly there.' *Then* a new immigrant, a carpenter from Glasgow, kissed not only the pretty stewardess who came in to greet us but also the customs official.

A few minutes before our arrival the loudspeaker in the El-Al plane began to broadcast the *hora*, the Jewish national dance. Two American ladies, who had spoken with a

9

mid-Western accent, hummed the tune discreetly. When we touched down, a few people applauded. It is a habit of the French to applaud particularly smooth landings; but these passengers were not concerned with the professional skill of the pilot, they were applauding the moment of arrival on the soil of Israel. Yet, the applause remained somewhat tentative, not quite sure of itself.

Why? What had happened between my journeys? I knew part of the answer before setting out on this trip. As a result of my first journey I had published a little book on Israel, called *Milk and Honey*. Now, two decades later, this book was like the Bible – quite good reading still, but definitely out of date. (I should add, in defence of my professional reputation, that while the Bible is the work of diverse hands, I wrote *Milk and Honey* singlehanded.) Some friends had suggested that I should bring the book up to date, but my publisher and I had agreed that conditions in Israel had changed so much that it would be simpler and better to write a completely new book. Hence my journey.

Revisiting Israel in 1957, soon after the Suez War, I had been aware of great changes; and the newspapers had informed me of others. Israel, in the first two decades of her existence, ceased to be a joke and became more and more like an ordinary country. During my 1949 visit the first railway line was opened between Haifa and Tel-Aviv and I heard at least 200 times the jocular remark that no Jew had driven a railway engine for 2,000 years. The man who did drive it after this interval, might have been a former gynaecologist turned engine driver; the waiter who served you in the restaurant in those days might have previously been a wholesale merchant of artificial silk or a lawyer; the fellow who drove your bus had been, perhaps, a major in the Polish Army. But even by 1957 all this had changed and few people were still amused by the sight of a Jew driving a train. This was a Jewish state, so why should the engine driver be a Seventh Day Adventist? By that time the waiter, too, was likely to be just a waiter, the bus driver just a bus driver and gynaecologists were sure to be treating women and not driving trains.

These, however, had been slow and natural changes. The most fundamental and dramatic changes occurred later, immediately after the Six Day War. Before that conflict Israel was a tiny country of two and a half million people, threatened with extermination by her hundred million Arab neighbours. That single week transformed Israel into a Great Power, on the verge of founding an Empire; Israel became a huge camp of two and a half million militarists, threatening her hundred million innocent, peaceful and defenceless neighbours with military occupation or worse. It was this amazing metamorphosis that cramped the style of my fellow-passengers and made the man sitting next to me, an attorney from Atlanta, Georgia, decidedly melancholy.

* * *

'You needn't be surprised,' I was told on the evening of my arrival by an old friend, 'the world does not like the idea of heroic Jews. But to hell with the world. We *are* and mean to remain aggressive Jews, able to stand up for ourselves and fight for our lives if we must. The world prefers us as peddlers; it tolerates us as successful bankers and even as famous concert-pianists. But Jews should not win military victories.'

'You may be right,' I told him, 'but this still does not explain why you forget all about the art of propaganda. Why do you let people go on believing that you wantonly attacked a bunch of peaceful Arabs, determined only to cultivate their gardens and mind their own business?'

'We don't care about the world,' he said. 'Before June 1967 everyone sympathized with us and felt strongly for us. They watched the approaching genocide with deep sympathy in their hearts and tears in their eyes. They were ready to send warm clothing to the 3,000 surviving Jewish children. But we did not call on their generosity for two reasons. Firstly, Israel is a warm country and no one needs warm clothing. Secondly, we beat the Arabs. After all this, we do not really care if the world shakes its head with moral indignation and is stupid enough to call us aggressors. Ours was the aggression of the ox who refused to enter the slaughter-house. Well, whether the world likes it or not, we have become a Land of Warriors and ceased to be a Land of Peddlers; or a Land of Prophets.'

These were bitter words. He was not alone in holding such views but he was not really representative of the general mood of the country. Most Israelis know that they were not really alone in the hour of their trial and that a small country is in desperate need of powerful allies. Besides, I also found out that the Prophets of Israel are not yet quite extinct. The prophet motive dies hard. This war turned the Israelis not only into a race of Warriors but once again into a land of Prophets. I heard the story of a rich gentleman of Afghanistan by the name of Daniel, who more than half a century ago astonished all his friends and countrymen by giving up his properties and other possessions and moving to Palestine with his parents, his wife and small children. 'We ought to live in the Jewish state,' he declared. 'What Jewish state?' his best friend asked him. His astonishment may be understood, as this man came to Palestine several years before the Balfour Declaration. Yet, he told them: 'We are Jews and we shall have our own country.' He came, settled down and started making a new fortune in his new homeland. A few years later his parents died and he – following an ancient tradition – had them buried on the Mount of Olives. Several decades passed, he became an old man himself and at the end of 1966 fell gravely ill. The same old friend who while still in Afghanistan had doubted his wisdom about the Jewish state, but who, nevertheless, had emigrated with him to the Promised Land, gently reminded him that he ought to buy a burial place for himself.

'But we have a burial place,' old Daniel informed his friend. 'Where?'

'On the Mount of Olives, of course, where my parents are buried.'

'But that belongs to Jordan.'

'It belongs to Jordan now. But by the time I die the Mount of Olives will be ours and I shall be buried there.'

'Daniel,' said his old friend, 'you are a good man and a clever man. But you are mad.'

Daniel died at the end of June, 1967. He was the first Jew to be buried in the Mount of Olives for almost twenty years. The Arab who dug his grave was the grandson of the man who had dug the grave of his parents.

*　　*　　*

One morning soon after my arrival I met the attorney from Atlanta, Georgia, in the lobby of our hotel. He walked up to me.

'I've heard a joke which worries me,' he said.

'It couldn't have been a very good joke,' I replied.

'It *is* a good joke but it worries me. And it worries me even more that people are repeating it here.'

'Let's hear it!'

'Two Jews, the famous Cohn and Green, haven't met for many years. Now they suddenly catch sight of each other in the middle of the Mediterranean: Cohn – obviously a new immigrant – is on the deck of one boat going to Israel, and Green, who is leaving Israel, is on the deck of the other. They eye each other with amazement and then shout across to each other at one and the same time:

'*Bist du meshugge?* . . . Are you quite mad?'

The attorney stopped and looked at me gravely.

'Who was right?' he asked me.

'I think Cohn was,' I answered. 'But I cannot be sure. You see, the whole purpose of my visit to Israel is to find out the answer to your question.'

If you, Gentle Reader, are also interested to know whether Mr Cohn or Mr Green was *meshugge*, please go on reading.

GM.

1 THE COUNTRY

Jewish Understatement

Nothing much has changed at Lydda, except that now it is called Lod. Tel-Aviv airport is still the only airport in the world where each passenger is met by ten relatives.

Have the Israelis changed in one important respect, I wondered? Have they become just a shade more modest or are they still full of true admiration for themselves? Their achievements, I knew, were considerable; but their own admiration for them used to be greater still. It was no formal, empty courtesy when they patted themselves on the back. Their eyes lit up whenever this one subject was mentioned: Israel. Their admiration was not put on; it was no affectation: they genuinely loved and revered themselves. There was no need – I recalled – for any visitor to utter courteous little phrases about the Land: his hosts did all that was needed for him. I remembered that just before my last visit, ten years before, the new Concert Hall had been built. Scores – no, hundreds – of people asked me: 'Have you seen the new Concert Hall? It's the finest in the world.' I always answered that I had not yet seen it, upon which they offered to transport me there without a moment's delay. While interested in the new Concert Hall, I nevertheless resisted all temptation: it was my greatest and proudest achievement in Israel that I managed not to see the new Concert Hall (the finest in the world).

My travelling companion on the present journey, knowing nothing of this Israeli habit, put her foot in it a few minutes after our arrival. She liked Tel-Aviv at first sight but she saw it for what it was, and as we drove into the city she started to say to the couple who had picked us up at the airport: 'An ugly town, like Tel-Aviv. . . .'

'What do you mean?' asked the man who drove the car.

My friend is no coward. She is used to sticking up for her views, however unpopular; she has often found herself in a minority of one, yet has spoken her mind bravely. But this time such a stand was impossible. This 'what do you mean?' expressed such a mixture of horror, pained surprise and utter incomprehension that it would have been downright rudeness, verging on inhumanity, to offend kind people who were doing us a favour.

'What I mean is that Tel-Aviv's beauty is not conspicuous, is it? Not that it is hidden, mind you, of course it isn't . . . but . . . how shall I put it? . . . it's all of its own. . . . It's not a *commonplace* beauty, it is really unique.'

Her explanation was accepted gracefully. Of course, if all she meant by asserting that Tel-Aviv was an ugly town was that its beauty was unique, that was different.

We reached the centre of the city and the driver pointed out a building to me: 'Have you seen the new Concert Hall? It is the finest in the world.'

Emotion flooded my heart. I felt that I had come home.

*   *   *

With this disposition for bragging it is amazing that few people gloat over the defeat of the Arabs. The Israelis are glad they won – the alternative would have been death; they are proud of their victory and grateful to 'the boys'. But they are not a warlike nation and they do not laugh at the Arabs. We shall see later on that the Arab refusal to sit down and talk peace with Israel is causing a hardening of the Israeli attitude and strengthens the rightist, 'not-a-square-inch-back!' element in the country, but this is not gloating or vainglory. Indeed, the silliest remark I heard was aimed not against the Arabs but against the British: 'The British hate us now because they envy us. They have lost an Empire and we have founded one.'

*   *   *

I said in my earlier book, and find no reason for retracting my statement, that the famous Jewish sense of humour got lost in transit to Israel. The simple truth is that all Israelis are Jewish; yet, Israel is not a Jewish country. Israel is a new, independent state, with growing self-confidence and a newly acquired national conscience. The Israeli sense of humour is more reminiscent of the sense of humour of Ghana, Zambia or Upper Volta – none of them truly renowned – than of the famous, wise, self-derogatory, warm and all-embracing sense of humour of Central European Jewry.

There is nothing surprising in this. The famous Jewish sense of humour was a defence-mechanism. Russian Jews were oppressed, kicked around and persecuted; their only weapon was to see their tormentor – the *muzhiks*, the small bureaucrats, the bullying army officers – for what they were: stupid, conceited, vain, uneducated and corrupt. They *had* to laugh at them to survive. But other qualities are needed for survival in the new surroundings of Israel. In Russia, and later in Central Europe, they had to learn to laugh at themselves in a half-apologetic manner. But there is nothing apologetic about Israel. The old Jews of Central Europe always felt that they had to justify their existence and apologize for being alive; the Israelis firmly believe that they have as much right to live as anyone else. The famous Jewish sense of humour was a minority-giggle; in Israel the Jews are not a minority any longer. Most Jewish jokes used to start with the immortal formula: 'Two Jews are travelling in a train. . . .' As soon as *all* the travellers in all the trains are Jews, the old Jewish joke dies a natural death.

*　　*　　*

With the tendency to take yourself dreadfully seriously, goes a great deal of touchiness. I ought to have known better what Israeli self-criticism amounts to, but still I made bad mistakes. There is just as keen a rivalry between Tel-Aviv and Jerusalem as there is between Rome and Florence or between Sydney and Melbourne. Humanity exhibits a general tendency (apart from

17

a small minority) to believe that the actual place where one lives is the *only* place one can live in. This tendency is most pronounced in Jerusalem and Tel-Aviv. An ardent local patriot of Jerusalem explained to me at great length that Tel-Aviv was a loud and vulgar place, quite unbearable. Jerusalem, on the other hand, was elegant and dignified. Tel-Aviv was ugly, Jerusalem was beautiful. Tel-Aviv was always hot, Jerusalem – at least at night – was always cool. And so on. In the end, more to please him than to express my true feelings, I nodded and said: 'Yes, if I came to live in Israel, I would certainly live in Jerusalem.'

He looked at me with fiery eyes and thundered: 'Why, what's wrong with Tel-Aviv?'

Once I had an argument, punctuated with ejaculations of pain and surprise, heavenward glances of mock tolerance and tight-lipped suffering because I maintained that the French Riviera was *deservedly* more popular and indeed much more beautiful than Tiberias. And so on, I could continue. This somewhat puerile Israeli love of boasting and praising everything Israeli, obviously often clashes with similar American tendencies. A friend of mine, a successful writer, playwright and film-producer, who counts, I believe, as a fairly rich man even in America but who is also as ardent an Israeli patriot as anyone else I know, visited the United States, where an American businessman asked him patronisingly, over a dry Martini: 'Why on earth do you go back to that place? What can you do there? Why don't you come and settle in America?'

My friend looked at him coolly and replied: 'My heart draws me to America but what can I do? The big money is in Israel.'

*   *   *

'Our sense of humour is really British,' a young man told me. 'Our true style of expression is the understatement.'

I could hardly believe my ears.

'Understatement?' I repeated incredulously.

He nodded.

'But how can you say that?' I asked him. 'Five minutes ago, when describing Israel, you used the adjectives wonderful, inimitable, admirable, superlative and matchless.'

He looked at me with surprise.

'Still an understatement,' he said coldly.

Vae Victoribus!

The intensity of Israeli self-admiration has not changed; but almost everything else has. Israel has gone through a traumatic, and subsequently a revealing, experience and these two events have changed her outlook on most matters.

I am not speaking of the Six Day War. That was a swift and dramatic campaign. Psychologically both its preliminaries and its aftermath were more important than the war itself. The fortnight preceding the war was much more frightening than the campaign: Nasser demanded the withdrawal of the United Nations Peacekeeping Force. U Thant, in one of the most stupefying acts in UN history (full of stupefying acts) obliged. When the moment came to fulfil the very task for which these UN troops had been sent there in the first place, they packed up and left. 'If you expect my peace-keeping force to keep the peace,' U Thant implied, 'you are badly mistaken.' Nasser closed the Straits of Tiran, Arabs massed on all Israel's frontiers, Arab radios and newspapers spat fire, talking of annihilation and hinting – with barely disguised joy – at the massacres to come, and meanwhile the Russians egged them on. The rest of the world, overcome by genuine sympathy, got ready to shed tears, write disapproving letters to *The Times* and send toys to the surviving Jewish children. (As they sent toys to the surviving Aberfan children, where, alas, the whole story was that hardly any children survived.)

Then came the kiss of death. A kiss more fatal than any kiss of Cleopatra's; more costly than any of Madame Pompadour's; and fraught with more danger than any of Mata Hari's. Only the kiss Judas gave to Jesus exceeds it in importance; only *that* kiss had more far-reaching consequences. I am talking of the kiss King Hussein and President Nasser planted on each other's face. The courtship leading up to this passionate scene was rather one-sided because Nasser kept repeating what he thought of Hussein but Hussein remained discreetly silent. The romantic dialogue went something like this:

NASSER: He [Hussein] ruled like a tyrant over the Jordanian people. . . . The King of Jordan . . . deceived his people, bowed to imperialism and opened his country to its dangers.

HUSSEIN: (Smiles shyly.)

NASSER: The King of Jordan is an agent of colonialism.

HUSSEIN: (Rubs his ears.) Did someone say something?

NASSER: King Hussein began last year to wag his tail. . . . The matter is that he wanted a few piastres from King Feisal.

HUSSEIN: (Looks in the other direction.)

NASSER: The rulers of Jordan have returned to their former methods of robbery, treachery and of serving the agents of imperialism.

HUSSEIN: (Smiles, somewhat self-consciously.)

NASSER: A traitor remains a traitor and he who sells himself once will always be ready to sell himself again. This applies to King Hussein. The King has sold himself to the imperialists and he marches together with them. It is impossible for us to trust him.

HUSSEIN: I love you too, Abdul. (They fall into each other's arms and kiss passionately.)

(All the above quotations come from Egyptian broadcasts.)

After the outbreak of the war and *after* the destruction of all the Arab air forces Hussein attacked Israel. Thus he ruined Jordan but saved himself. He could and did survive the Arab defeat, however disastrous it was to his country; he could never have survived an Arab victory in which he had failed to participate.

*　　*　　*

After the war Israel could breathe again. They expected praise and admiration, warm handshakes and congratulations. They did receive some grudging admiration even from Russia; but warmth and panegyrics were conspicuously absent. Indeed, soon after the end of the war, we started hearing and reading stories about Israeli atrocities, burnt-down and blown-up houses, bulldozed villages, and the heroic fight of El Fatah. We saw innumerable pictures of Arab refugees (who, of course, deserve sympathy). The world was puzzled; and Israel was even more puzzled.

Nasser complained that the Israeli planes had attacked from a westerly direction while he and his air-staff confidently expected them to attack from the east or, in the worst case, from the north. This act of Israel's could not be reconciled with the rules of the famous Imperialist game; in other words, it wasn't cricket. Some military commentators (including certain British) accused the Israelis of 'concealing their real strength'. This meant that had poor Nasser known he was heading for a swift and humiliating defeat instead of an easy victory, he would not have attacked; he was a victim of Jewish cunning and trickery. Israel was getting a bad press all over the world and even in the friendliest circles heads were shaken. Even Jews in Europe and America were heard to utter anti-semitic remarks. It slowly dawned on the Israelis that it was one thing to be the underdog and quite another to be the mighty victor. It suddenly became the story of huge ruthless David bullying poor little innocent and defenceless Goliath.

Israel also deprived the world of its chance of shedding tears of genuine sympathy over her destruction. The world resents this; it likes to feel noble and sympathetic. An Israeli politician put it succinctly: 'We win the war and lose your sympathy. It's too bad but we'd rather have it this way.' One newspaper editor had another theory: 'After World War II a wave of philosemitism swept over the world. We Jews had suffered too much and everyone felt sorry for us. But this is an unnatural state of things; now the world can sigh with relief. The era of philosemitism is over. We have won this war and the world is free to dislike us again.'

While the Arabs are spending millions of pounds on propaganda, the Israelis have decided not to be provocative and not to rub it in. The victors, cap in hand, sued for peace. Their defeated adversaries turned away with scorn. The expansionist element in Israel sighed with relief: no peace, no withdrawal from the occupied territories. The Arabs still demand unconditional surrender from the people who beat them. Israel has, at last, got the message: *Vae Victoribus!* Woe to the Victors!

The Six Day War was easy; it is this Seventh Day that is very, very difficult. Israel must live with this thought. For the time being, she must go on playing the role of the ruthless imperialist power and it is Hussein who must repeat for some time to come the ancient Jewish prayer: 'Next year in Jerusalem!'

How Well Off?

'Is the country rich or poor?' I asked one of Israel's economic experts.

'That depends,' he replied thoughtfully.

'Depends on what?'

'Whether you want me to speak for internal or external consumption. For internal consumption we are miserably poor and in dire need; we have always to prepare our people for a rise in taxation. For external consumption our situation is rosy; this is because we want foreign investment.'

'There must be such a thing as reality,' I suggested.

'There isn't,' my friend shook his head firmly. 'Not in economics.'

'Our standard of living,' he went on, 'has reached the level of the poorer countries in Western Europe. We are not so well off as Switzerland, Holland or Sweden, but we have reached the standards of Austria, Italy or the poorer parts of France.'

He added ruefully: 'We are going to introduce television in a few weeks from now. Then we shall, most unfortunately, have everything a modern country can dream of. The truth is that our standard of living has trebled since 1949.'

This was obvious to me who, in fact, visited Israel in that very year. Britain was then the land of austerity, while Israel had the *tsena* – the same in Hebrew. Both austerity and *tsena* have been forgotten by now, yet a close parallel between the British and Israeli economy persists. Both countries have been plagued with balance of payment troubles and by creeping inflation; by the excessive power of Trade Unions in a capitalist society; by the Unions' ability to apply pressure at the most inconvenient times; by a stop-go economy; and also by the periodical unemployment that goes with this.

The reasons for the creeping inflation in Israel are threefold: (1) an unnaturally high defence budget (the highest in the world per head of population); (2) high investments (which do not bring an *immediate* rise in production); and (3) German reparations. These reparations meant that too much money was chasing too few goods. This last problem has been more or less solved by now, by restrictions imposed upon the German money actually coming into the country.

Israel is becoming more and more industrialized – thirty-five per cent of the population are engaged in industry – but, my economist friend told me, new industries must be introduced or developed without delay.

'Everybody knows how to produce textiles, plastic mugs and shoes,' he told me. 'The most backward countries do it. We need electronic industries, metallurgy, chemical, motor and aircraft industries. We cannot cut down on defence. So we must produce arms – and once we produce them we might as well sell them to others.'

The rise in the standard of living does not mean that life in Israel is easy. People have to work hard, often in two jobs, and nearly all the women are at work. Motor-cars are extremely expensive, yet more and more people can afford them. The washing-machine era has arrived. As for television, Israel resisted bravely for a long time but she had to succumb, largely for political reasons. Jordan, Egypt and Lebanon all have television services and the entire Arab population of Israel – Israeli Arabs as well as the newly conquered ones – keep watching these stations. This is permitted, no one has ever thought of stopping them. One can see Israeli officers having meals in Arab restaurants on the West Bank while the Arab proprietors and guests sit watching – say – King Hussein's return from one of his numerous visits abroad. Hussein tells his people that his journey has been a great success, the hour of revenge is near now and Israel will be wiped off the map. The Arab masses in Jordan cheer; the Arabs in the restaurant watch silently, with inscrutable faces but definitely with a 'we have heard

25

this before' air. The Israeli officers – who understand every word – pay their bills and go, not unduly perturbed. Nevertheless, the Israeli government has thought it wise to counteract all this propaganda and give the Arabs another television diet.

But it is not Arabs alone who watch the Jordanian, Egyptian and Lebanese programmes. American tourists watch them too. The watching habit seems to be compulsive. In a *kibbutz* – which also runs a hotel – I saw some two dozen American tourists watching a funny show from Beirut. A fat Arab, wearing a Turkish fez, cracked rapid jokes *à la* Bob Hope or Groucho Marx. The Lebanese studio-audience roared with laughter and the Americans in the *kibbutz* roared with them. All this simply confirmed an old suspicion of mine : if you do not understand a television programme you are bound to enjoy it ; if you do understand it—well, that's a different matter.

Israel is getting along all right and she – a small and not too rich nation – finds it possible to support developing countries in Asia and Africa. This last mentioned activity is connected with Israel's geographical mobility – a completely new notion. Sometimes Israel is a European country in the Middle East ; on other occasions she is a Mediterranean country and nothing to do with Europe ; then again, she is part of the Middle East. 'What I like about Israel,' an African diplomat, having Israel's help to developing countries in mind, told me, 'is that she accepts her Asian destiny.'

'Quite,' I nodded.

Israel has a socialist government and a capitalist economy – not unusual in our modern world. I complained about this to a friend, remarking that it is sad to see it here, too, manufacturers of shoddy and useless goods growing rich and – worse still – to see real-estate speculators reaping rich rewards for doing nothing.

'This part,' my friend replied, 'is even worse in Israel than anywhere else. Here the speculators thrive as anywhere else. But, you see, this is the Holy Land. And here the land goes up not only in value, not only in price but also – lucky devils – in holiness. Believe it or not, it is thirty-five per cent holier than ten years ago.'

* * *

'I like the Arabs and don't like the Jews,' a Briton told me in Tel-Aviv. He used to occupy a high position in the British diplomatic service and I took his utterance to be a manifestation of that pro-Arab and anti-Jewish bias which is reputed to be not uncommon in the Foreign Office. 'I served in many Arab countries,' he contined. 'I wouldn't trust the average Arab; I wouldn't believe one word he tells me. But I like the Arabs and dislike the Jews.'

'Where were your sympathies during the Six Day War?' I asked him.

He looked at me with surprise.

'Fully and unreservedly with the Jews. I am not talking about politics.'

His statement struck me as strange and biased at first, but soon I understood only too well what he meant. As I shall have to speak frequently of the 'Arabs' in this book – thus lumping together one hundred million human beings – I might as well say a few words about my attitude towards them.

The Arabs are attractive and likeable people. They ooze charm and I do not mean this in a derogatory sense; it comes naturally to them, it is not at all affected. There is a great deal we can learn from them, Israelis and Europeans alike. Family ties are sacred for the Arabs; they bow to their elders and treat them with respect – not an unattractive quality in an age which has developed a silly veneration of youth. Arab hospitality is also a noble and civilized trait in a world growing more and more mercenary every day.

Israelis do not know the Arabs. Most of them have never exchanged a single word with a single Arab. 'Arabs' are a distant – sometimes not so distant – threat to them, having to do with abstract politics and not with everyday life. In spite of this, many Israelis tend to despise them as backward people. Those who know them have more respect for them. The Arabs are as intelligent as the Jews. In fact, these two Semitic peoples resemble each other as closely as the Scots resemble the English, and resent just as much having this similarity pointed out. The Arabs spent long centuries under Turkish oppression – which is not too good for any nation – and subsequently their own feudal rulers oppressed, exploited and fooled them in the most cynical way. So the Jews, no doubt, are a few generations ahead of them, at the moment. But a few generations means nothing in history. The two peoples must learn to know each other because – whether they like it or not – they will have to live together.

'The real trouble is that the Arabs are completely unreliable. They are all born liars. You cannot trust them,' this is the customary rejoinder shared even by my British diplomat friend who liked the Arabs very much. But Arabs do not hate the truth, they simply have an Oriental approach to reality. They are natural wishful thinkers, not natural liars. They look at something green and call it red; not because they want to mislead you but because it used to be red in the old days when the Arabs were a great people, the most civilized on earth. They wish it was still red, so they *see* it red, so it *is* red. Life is not as it is but as it ought to be. As it used to be in the great days. Reality is *my* relation to facts, consequently reality depends as much on me as it depends on so-called facts. This way of looking at things enabled Nasser to turn his resounding defeat of 1956 into a famous victory as far as he and the Arab world were concerned; it enables Arabs to see every disaster as a new triumph. This philosophy does not lead to riches; but it may lead to happiness.

The desert is endless; and also timeless. If you are unable to look certain facts in the face today, you may always convince yourself that they will be different in 300 years – as it was very different 3,000 years ago. What is 300 years, anyway? Or 3,000? And who will be here to tell whether things have, in fact, changed or not in 300 years?

The Arabs are a very proud people; the Jews are not proud. The Jews are practical, logical and insist on their rights; they are often arrogant but they are not proud. They are sober, self-assertive realists. The Arabs are proud dreamers. In a way they are both right as, indeed, both sides often are right in this tragic conflict; for the Arabs dreams *are* reality; but the Jews know that present-day reality is not a dream.

The Arabs love to express themselves in parables. Here

follows one which well describes their relationship to reality.

An old Arab is sitting at the end of the village where a large group of noisy children is playing. The old man calls one child and asks him: 'Why are you wasting your time here when figs are being distributed free of charge at the other end of the village?' The boy looks at him incredulously but he passes on this information to an older boy. After some whispering, first one then another child disappears, until all of them are gone. Peace reigns: the old man sits smoking his *narghile* in the blissful tranquillity. But suddenly he exclaims: 'Oh Allah! What am I doing here, wasting my time, when figs are being distributed at the other end of the village?'

He jumps up and runs to the other end of the village to get his share of the figs.

* * *

And now let us return to the economic situation. If the Arab masses – workers and peasants – are better off than they used to be, the situation of the professional and upper classes is much worse. A doctor in Jordan could make about 100 times as much as an ordinary, unskilled labourer (£1,000 versus £10 per month). The gap has now been narrowed. The worker earns much more than before, but still not enough; the doctor can still make ends meet though his earnings have been severely cut. The result is that the professional and upper classes persuade the workers that *they* are unhappy and miserable too and, further, they are traitors to their country and the Arab cause if they dare see anything good in Israeli occupation. I do not suggest that Arab workers and peasants love the Israelis or are pleased to have them in their country; but all workers, peasants (and shopkeepers, doctors, sanitary engineers, butchers and aristocrats) prefer to make more money rather than less. So these poor people see a point in Israeli occupation; though they have to act as if they did not.

There are two main grievances one hears about on the West Bank of the Jordan: (1) Arab banks are not allowed to reopen and (2) Arab vegetables and other market products – much cheaper than Israeli products – are not allowed into Israel, not even into Jerusalem.

(1) On June 7, 1967, the Israeli Military Commander ordered all the banks on the West Bank to close. No one quarrelled with this decision, not even the banks, who thus avoided a rush on them which would have rendered them unable to meet their obligations. The trouble is that the banks have remained closed.

The head offices of the Arab banks are mostly in Amman; and two countries which are at war do not, as a rule, have a common banking system. But the Israelis and the Jordanians do have a common agricultural marketing system which works quite well, and they also share a common currency (Israeli pounds as well as Jordanian dinars are legal tender on the West Bank). Amman does not permit the Arab banks to re-open because banks represent economic power; they can decide who should have a loan and who not, and the Arabs are afraid of losing this control over their banks on Israeli territory. Depositors can go over to Jordan to draw limited sums from their accounts but that is all. The English banks who used to have branches on the West Side of the Jordan – fearing an Arab boycott – have also refused to re-open. They do as their Arab counterparts do, they say. The result is that the Israeli banks have opened branches in Jerusalem and on the West Bank and are doing well.

(2) The problem of vegetables and fruit is even simpler. The Arabs produce more cheaply and they want to sell their products in Israel. They can bring these products in from Jordan – from enemy territory – and sell them on the West Bank but they cannot export them into Jerusalem or Israel. The Israeli explanation is this:

'Jerusalem is part of Israel, so no distinction should be drawn between the two. It would be impossible to let these products into Jerusalem but not into Israel. On the other hand we cannot let the Arabs flood our whole country with cheap vegetable products.'

'But why not?' ask the Arabs. 'First of all, this would make life cheaper in Israel, which is allegedly one of the aims of the

31

government. Also, it is particularly unjust towards the Arabs who earn less than Israelis but have to pay the same taxes [indirect taxes, that is] from their lower incomes.'

When I put the Arab standpoint to some Israeli experts, they agreed that there was an element of injustice here, but letting these products in, they maintained, would mean the collapse of the entire agricultural price structure and would lead to the gravest trouble with the Histadruth – the Federation of Trade Unions – who are the main agricultural producers and marketers.

'Israel,' one of them said, 'is not the only country where a powerful agricultural lobby can exert undue pressure on the government. Have you never heard of such a thing? Do you come from Britain? Or from America?'

* * *

Many Arab shopkeepers are doing very well indeed. The tourist trade is thriving. Almost all Israelis have been to the newly occupied territories and thousands of foreign tourists flock there, too, at the expense of the old favourite tourist places which are being neglected. The souvenir trade is flourishing, Arab restaurants and antique shops do a roaring business. Immediately after the war, the Israelis discovered in the Arab shops many goods which were unavailable in Israel : ballpoint pens, cheap cameras, tape-recorders, binoculars and scores of smaller, attractive items. The news spread that the newly conquered territories were good for shopping and Israelis swarmed there to buy up whatever they could lay their hands on. The Arab shops, however, soon ran out of goods and could not replace them from China, Russia and East Germany. Yet, the demand was there. So the Arab shopkeepers went to Tel-Aviv, bought up all the junk they could find and sold it at exorbitant prices to visitors from Tel-Aviv who were delighted to get it. Which should be a lesson to politicians on how easy it is to make everybody happy.

Money

In *Milk and Honey* I reported that I found the monetary system of the land slightly confusing. I gave a purely factual account of the system which I reproduce here in abbreviated form:

'The Israeli Pound (I£) is the successor of the Palestine Pound (P£). An I£ is equivalent to a British Pound sterling.

'The main thing to remember is this. When they speak of a piastre they mean 10 mills; when they speak of a shilling they mean 50 prutoth; when an elderly gentleman says 'a franc', he really means five prutoth, i.e. a coin which does not exist at all (it is exactly like talking of a guinea). When the same elderly gentleman says 'a girsh' he means one fifth of a shilling and when he says 'a grusch' you are driven completely crazy.

'Yet, strange as it may seem, there is a clue to all this. An I£ is divided into 1,000 prutoth. Why? Do not ask me. That is the official decision and that should be the end of it. But the Israelis are an unofficially minded nation and prutoth (pruta, in singular) are just not mentioned. A pruta used to be called a mill in the times of the mandate. A mill is sometimes mentioned, but rarely. What they do mention often is the piastre which, however, does not exist. If it did, it would consist of ten mills and this supposition is the basis of the Israeli monetary system. Lest that be too simple for you, they also count in shillings, which also do not exist. If the shilling existed it would be five piastres, which does not exist, but if it did, five piastres would be fifty prutoth, but prutoth is never mentioned. It is obvious that even these difficulties could be mastered with will-power and perseverance. So some elderly people keep talking of girsh, which is Arabic for piastre (but piastre does not exist).

Yiddish speaking people will speak of a grusch. That is the easiest of all. Grusch is simply Yiddish for girsh which (just to refresh your memory) is Arabic for piastre which latter does not exist. If all this is now clear to you the only other thing to remember is that a franc is half a grush, i.e. five prutoth (which is never mentioned), i.e. half a girsh which does not exist.'

No one ever questioned the absolute precision of my account. Indeed, it was universally acknowledged that the whole complicated issue had never before been stated with such clarity and brevity. Yet, my account caused a certain consternation in Israel. They themselves were not responsible for any confusion, I was told; I ought to know how good the British were at creating a muddle. British Imperial muddle was second only to Turkish Ottoman muddle and the Israeli monetary system was an inheritance from both Turkish and British times.

Returning after twenty years, I found the monetary system completely reformed and put on a clear, cool, logical basis, worthy of the new state of Israel. The gist of the new system is this.

The new Israeli pound (I£) is called a lira which, however, does not exist. When currency reform was discussed a number of sentimental old people – remembering biblical times – wanted to call the monetary unit a shekel. This proposal was turned down by Parliament, consequently a number of people called the lira (which does not exist) a shekel which according to them ought to exist. Their justification is that Israel is a free country.

The smaller unit now is the agorat which, of course, is never mentioned, not even as a joke. People speak of prutoth, which survive from their previous period of non-existence. In all fairness, it is mostly old people who speak of prutoth. Young people call the agorat a grusch, which does not exist and no young person can possibly remember a time when it did exist. To simplify the system, five agorat is often called a shilling which does not exist either and will not exist even in Britain, for long.

(In the same spirit, all road signs in Jerusalem – even the

newly painted ones – give you the direction of and distances to the Mandelbaum Gate – which is always mentioned but does not exist.)

All I have to add to this is that the Israeli pound is no longer equivalent to the pound sterling. Although our own pound, after two devaluations and a lot of wear and tear, is considerably less sterling than it used to be, an Israeli pound is only about two shillings and sixpence. This is half of a crown – half of a British unit which does not exist. This is, by the way, one of the greatest British achievements in the field of muddle: in this case, two halves do not make a whole; two halves make five. And this, if nothing else, should teach the Israelis a little modesty.

Manners

We noticed some yellowish red liquid on a street vendor's stand and walked up to him.

'A glass of apple juice, please.'

He filled a glass and handed it to my companion.

'This is carrot juice. Much better for you.'

I was greatly embarrassed by this because I was just in the middle of telling her that manners had changed in Israel and was about to explain why this was bound to happen.

I shut up temporarily. We went to a restaurant for a dairy lunch (a popular and delicious meal) and to our joy we discovered on the menu a kind of goat cheese we both knew and loved from our Central European days. It was the cheapest and commonest of all cheeses. When we ordered it, the waitress shook her head.

'That's not good enough for you. I'll get you something much better.'

There was no appeal against her decision. She was an elderly female, very sweet, all smiles and kindness, and she was obviously venting her maternal instincts on us.

'At least,' I remarked to my companion when the waitress was out of ear shot, 'they all seem to care. They are concerned. They think of our well-being.'

I did feel a lingering doubt on this point. Perhaps, I thought, the street vendor had no apple juice and gave us the carrot juice instead – who knows? – not because he was worried lest apple did not contain enough vitamins for me but because he did not want to lose a customer; and maybe the waitress, for all her maternal instincts, merely wanted to sell us something more expensive. Who can see into the soul of another? In any case, I was determined to prove that Israeli manners had improved beyond recognition in the last twenty years.

'What is that story from your earlier book people keep mentioning?' my companion asked me. 'About a waiter and some cups of tea.'

'That's a thing of the past. Completely out of date now.'

I refused to repeat the story but she found a copy of *Milk and Honey* and read the story for herself.

'I was in a café with seven other people and a member of our party ordered "eight teas" for us. The waiter trotted back after a few minutes with glasses of steaming, purple tea on a tray and a slice of lemon in each glass. The waiter put the tray down, leaving the task of distributing the glasses to us. We did so and found one glass too many. My host called the waiter back and said to him:

"Look, we ordered eight glasses of tea and you brought us nine."

The waiter was unimpressed.

"*Nu*," he replied, "what about it? Another Yid will come and drink it."

The other Yid duly arrived and drank it.'

My companion read the story and I explained to her:

'This type of behaviour belongs to the past. It just doesn't exist any more.'

The same afternoon we went to interview a high-ranking civil servant who discussed problems of his department with me and then ordered refreshments.

'No doubt,' he said, 'you remember your own story about the waiter and those cups of tea. The very same thing happens three times a day in my office.'

On our way out my companion remarked: 'I thought you said that this sort of thing had completely disappeared.'

'What I meant was that a *waiter* would not behave like that nowadays. Members of the establishment making little jokes among themselves is an entirely different kettle of fish.'

Soon afterwards we were having coffee in a coffee bar. I took a box of saccharin tablets from my pocket and asked the lady: 'How many do you want? Two or three?' I shook the container rather more than I meant to and all the tablets fell out and rolled in all directions over the table and on to the floor. The waiter stood by, watching us pick them up and roaring with laughter.

'Two or three? . . . Ha-ha-ha. . . . Perhaps you meant two or three hundred, ha-ha-ha. . . .'

My companion rubbed it in. 'So it's not only members of the establishment who behave like that. . . .'

I admitted that this waiter's manners were somewhat informal. But why not? People – I said – were not deferential and humble any more and why should they be? There are no large differences of income, so people feel equal; they *are* equal. On top of it, these people had just come through some harrowing experiences together and those experiences had narrowed the gap between man and man. There were no doormen there – I continued – in front of the big hotels, wearing gold-braided admiral's uniforms; no waiters in tails, recalling Edwardian diplomats; neither could one find that chip-on-the-shoulder-chumminess which asserts aggressively that 'I'm as good as anyone else' when no one thinks of denying it. 'One man works in a restaurant as a waiter, the other is a judge or a general or a cabinet-minister – so what? A man is still a man.'

A good speech; and I delivered it rather impressively. But I knew that I was beaten. Israeli manners were just as bad as ever before. Israelis still keep teaching you your own business. God knows everything but the Israelis know everything better; they cannot bear to be wrong in anything. When you make a remark, they will interrupt you with 'of course, of course, of course . . .' meaning how silly it is to state the obvious at great length. Or cut you short with 'OK, OK, OK' – meaning more or less the same. If they cannot butt in, they make faces, showing that they have already got the point and there is no need for you to go on nattering.

They are quick-witted and always jump to conclusions. Often to wrong ones. On one occasion I went into a shoe-shop and began: 'Have you got . . .'

'A pair of brown shoes, like the ones in the window?'

'No. Have you got . . .'

'A pair of black?'

'No.'

'Suede?'

'No.'

'Sandals?'

'No.'

'Then have I got what?'

'Have you got a daughter called Susannah, because if you have I have a message for her from London.'

With all that impatience and quickness of mind, they always believe that you, on the other hand, must be pretty slow and dim. I stopped a man in the street in Haifa and asked him where Leon Blum Street was. He told me: 'Fourth on the right.' I thanked him and was about to proceed. He raised his hand, stopped me and told me, speaking with great emphasis, very loudly and very slowly: 'Not the first. Not the second. Not the third. The fourth.'

I thanked him again – somewhat dryly, this time – but I was still not allowed to go.

'Not on the left. On the right.'

*   *   *

I must add that whenever the average Israeli realises that he has found his match in rudeness, he takes it in manly fashion. My companion had some minor complaint and a doctor friend advised me on the telephone to buy certain tablets for her. I jotted down the name of the medicine in my illegible handwriting and later I read it out to the lady assistant in the chemist shop. She shouted at me: 'Give me that paper. I can read. I am not blind.'

I replied: 'It seems that you are not deaf either. So just listen.'

This improved our relationship and the rest of the transaction passed off without a hitch.

In spite of all these irritating and annoying little incidents and skirmishes, politeness is slowly gaining ground. You come across many acts of courtesy and consideration; motorists (sometimes) wait even two – or a maximum of three – seconds to let a pedestrian pass and extend minor courtesies to one another. The atmosphere is much more relaxed than on my first visit; there is no tension in the air; the rush is much less murderous. The new way of behaviour gaining ground – admittedly, rather slowly – is a matter-of-fact, no-fuss consideration of other people and not the old world courtesy, European courtier manners or the cool, disciplined and reserved English behaviour. But why should it not be so? I, for one, prefer a little genuine consideration to seven bows, let alone to the 'after-you-Cecil' type of courtesy.

* * *

A surveyor friend of mine was taken to a distant place in the country by his assistant. He used to know the place well but had not visited it for a few months while his assistant had been there almost every week.

'They are building a new military airport here,' my friend remonstrated with his assistant, 'and you did not even mention it to me?'

The assistant had his excuse ready: 'I am sorry. I did not know it was a secret.'

I encountered an even better version of Israeli secrecy. I was interviewing a high military gentleman and could not accept his explanations on a certain point. I pressed him hard. In the end he lost his patience and walked to his files cabinet.

'Very well,' he said angrily, 'this is top secret. But I'm going to show it to you.'

And he did.

On Books, Brandy and Rape

Israel is not an over-frivolous country. The national pastime is reading. This has not changed even after the influx of a very large number of Oriental Jews, many of whom were illiterate when they arrived. I had a look into a slum dwelling in Tel-Aviv – perhaps the poorest and most miserable room I ever saw in Israel – and saw in that dismal basement a very old man, lying on his belly on a ramshackle iron bedstead. A few inches away from his nose he held a book – which was falling to pieces – and with the help of a magnifying glass he was reading with avid interest, under the solitary, bare bulb that hung on its long wire. Perhaps you do not find Nietzsche and the collected novels of Dostoevsky in *every* unskilled labourer's home – as you did twenty years ago – but you find more people reading worthwhile books than anywhere else.

Near my Tel-Aviv hotel, in Yarkon Street, there is a little park, separated from the street by a low brick wall. On that wall there sat every day a casual labourer, a Yemenite or Iraqi Jew, waiting for something to turn up, perhaps a chance of carrying a few suitcases or peeling some potatoes in one of the hotels. He was listening, whenever I passed, to his transistor radio. Not to pop-music – as most men like him would everywhere else in the world – but to news and political talks. The broadcasts were in Hebrew, so I did not understand them but I kept hearing the names of the American President, and Vietnam, and de Gaulle and Kosygin and Dubček. Once I asked an Israeli friend who was walking with me, what the man was listening to: it was a review of the foreign press. Was it possible, I asked myself, that this was the country's real

strength? Was it possible that the army could fight as well as it did precisely because casual labourers, sitting on low brick walls, were more interested in the leading article of *Le Monde* than in the Rolling Stones?

This devotion to culture can be carried too far, I thought, when I noticed that my taxi driver kept reading his newspaper while driving. Fortunately, it was a rather uneventful, indeed dull, day; the news was not absorbing, so we reached our destination.

Night clubs in Israel are few and far between. When I remarked to one or two friends that Israel could not hold a candle to Las Vegas, I meant it as a compliment but they were deeply hurt. You cannot deride anything Israeli just like that. But I must repeat it now: if it is gay, ribald and lascivious night-life you are after, Israel is not the place for you. The night clubs you do find are nearer in spirit to a YMCA than to dens of inquity.

By the way, speaking of the YMCA: one can find in Jerusalem the only Young Men's Christian Association in the whole world where most of the members are Jews. (Their proportion has gone down lately. After the War a lot of Moslems joined.)

Another grave problem in Israel is alcoholism. The trouble is that people do not drink enough alcohol. There are no pubs; one can get drinks in the bars of hotels, in restaurants and cafés but few Israelis drink anything stronger than beer. They drink cold fruit juice but less of even that than before. When I first visited Israel *gazoz* – various aerated fruit juices – was the national drink. Millions of gallons of *gazoz* were consumed every day and I quoted a story then current in Israel. A Christian and a Jew get lost in the desert. They are found after many days of search and when, at last, the rescue party arrives, they hear the Christian shouting: 'Water! Water!' and the Jew: '*Gazoz! Gazoz!*'

This time I did not once hear the expression *gazoz*. It has become simply 'fruit juice' and that Jewish gentleman, lost in the desert would today, I suspect, accept a glass of water, provided it was properly iced.

The low alcohol consumption worries the government

because they are trying to develop – or rather increase – wine production on Mount Carmel. Israel is the only country in the world where official propaganda tries to persuade the population to drink more:

WINE MAKES YOUR FOOD TASTE BETTER!

Israel produces a brandy of her own. A precious friendship with an Israeli was nipped in the bud because I suggested that some of the top French brandies were a shade better, but Israeli brandy is quite drinkable and people are gently prodded:

A LITTLE BRANDY MAKES YOU MERRIER!

But it is no use. They do not want to be merry. They prefer to remain gloomy; and sober. Passover is the great time of the wine trade: everyone is supposed to drink four glasses of wine per day, for eight days. And they do so: they are prepared to drink as a religious duty; but not for pleasure.

* * *

Do not, however, believe for a moment that this habit of abstention is regarded as a virtue. On the contrary, it is regarded by many people as proof that the Jews are not really alive, are unable to enjoy life properly and are not really human. They just cannot win.

Even their decency in another field is sometimes turned against them. I heard a French journalist questioning some Arabs in Gaza about Jewish atrocities during the war. Gaza – as we shall see – is a place of bitterness, hatred and frustration and there are few charges the local Arabs would hesitate to level against the Jews. The Frenchman asked an Arab teacher, who was only too willing to describe atrocities which had never occurred in great and lurid detail, about cases of rape.

'What rape?' asked the Arab.

'Well. You know. Rape. The Israeli army raping Arab women.'

The Arab teacher shook his head and declared there had been no rape.

45

'What? No rape at all?'

'No,' replied the Arab apologetically and obviously hating the idea that he had to disappoint the friendly Frenchman. 'No rape at all.'

The Frenchman raised his eyes to heaven and exclaimed with contempt: 'Oh God! And they call *that* an army!'

Language

Israel has learnt Hebrew between my visits.

She has learnt Hebrew in three instalments. In the beginning, as is well known, no one, not a single soul under the sun, spoke Hebrew. It is the only successful revival of a dead language in modern times, indeed, ever; neither the Irish, nor the Welsh have succeeded half as well. The revival of Hebrew was essentially the brainchild and work of one man, Ben Yehuda, who lived from 1858 to 1922. In his youth he was a student at the Russian university of Dvinsk. He emigrated to Palestine and refused to talk to his wife, children and all strangers, except in Hebrew. 'I don't say a Zionist must be insane,' said President Weizmann, 'but it helps if he is.' Indeed, Ben Yehuda was for long regarded as raving mad by many. But the habit of talking Hebrew caught on and achieved the impossible. 'To have one's own language is the root of human dignity,' wrote Aristotle and Ben Yehuda agreed with him. Today milkmen and tailors, bureaucrats and greengrocers, postmen and lawyers speak Hebrew. Some speak it well, some indifferently, some badly – but they speak it as naturally as French or Persian is spoken.

Ben Yehuda himself derived his knowledge of Hebrew from the Bible. In the case of other languages, a great literary work is a by-product of the language; in this case, the language is the by-product of a great literary work.

Hebrew (if I may repeat briefly what I said in *Milk and Honey*) is a very difficult language because it is written without vowels. As though in English, let us say, the national anthem were to be written thus:

Gd sv r nbl Qn,
Gd sv r grcs Qn,
Gd sv th Qn.

Take the English word: *dog*. If the English had adopted the Hebrew way of spelling (and considering the kind of spelling they *did* adopt, it would have been but a small step further) *dog* would be written dg. In this sentence: *th dg ws brkng ldly* (provided you knew that the rest of the words meant *the . . . was barking loudly*) you would jump to the conclusion that dg, in this context stood for *dog*. After all, you would naïvely ask, who would bark loudly, but a dog? But *dg*, in a vowelless spelling, could stand for many things: *dig, dag, dug, Doge, Dago, edge, adage* and *adagio*. In a music critic's notice the above sentence might well be read 'the adagio was barking loudly'. Wll, wll, wll. . . .

There were other difficulties, too, A language resuscitated from an ancient book was more suitable for expressing Biblical oaths than racy modern thoughts or problems of technology. A further serious handicap was that no one was really good at Hebrew. At the time of my first visit Israel's population was about a million. One third of these people had arrived in the country in the previous eighteen months which – proportionately – would have meant fifteen million immigrants and refugees in Britain and forty-five million in the United States – all ignorant of English and all arriving within a year and a half. The average knowledge of Hebrew was so feeble that a peculiar job existed in Israel in those days: a gentleman, who really knew the language well, went through the speeches of members of parliament, including ministers, corrected them and freed them of major grammatical mistakes, thus rendering them publishable in their equivalent of Hansard.

Less than a decade later – during my second visit – Israel reached stage number two, and seemed to be the country where more languages were spoken more badly than anywhere else in the world. Many Central Europeans spoke bad German; Rumanians and Bulgarians spoke bad French; other Rumanians, as well as Slovaks and Croats spoke pidgin Hungarian; some Yugoslavs spoke bad Italian, some Italians spoke bad

Spanish; Greeks spoke bad Turkish, Turks spoke bad Greek; bad English was the second language of Israel and bad Hebrew, of course, remained the national language.

All this has changed by now – during stage number three. The majority of the population (just over fifty per cent, yet a majority) speak Hebrew as their mother tongue. The main progress, however, is not simply that more people speak it, but that so many people speak it absolutely naturally. It is not a great effort any more; neither is it a peculiarity, nor a joke: it is a language. The sale of Hebrew newspapers goes up as more and more people can *read* Hebrew, too. (It was paradoxical that in this most literate of countries there was a large number of people who could speak a kind of Hebrew but could not read it. The absence of vowels had defeated them.) Newly manufactured and naturally born words filled more and more gaps and these newcomers became living, organic parts of the language. There were some duds; some words failed to catch on but the language became richer almost every day.[1] In the sixties one could discourse upon any subject – technology, pop music, sex, art and science – as in any other tongue. Regional dialect has not been developed, the country is too small for that: one cannot tell a man of Dan from a man of Beersheba by his speech. But other dialects are flourishing: forensic, histrionic, military, scholastic, criminal, etc. At the time of my first visit, Hebrew had managed miraculously to *survive*; by the time of my last visit it *lived*.

My linguistic experiences in Israel destroyed an old theory of mine which I had always thought infallible. In the early fifties I visited Finland, a country I loved. I was especially

[1] The manufacturing of new words, thus turning ancient, biblical Hebrew into a modern tongue, was the task of the *Vaad ha-Lashon*, the Language Council. I mentioned this institution in my first book on Israel but misspelt it. In the course of twenty years I must have received a thousand letters correcting my spelling, the nearest coming from the same block of flats where I lived, the farthest from New Zealand. They all told me to correct this fault in the next edition but when new editions were printed I either knew nothing of it in advance or else could not find a single one of those numerous letters – so the misspelling persisted. The august body was recognized in the meantime (in 1954) as the official Academy of the Hebrew Language, whose rulings are final in matters of grammar and spelling. So I bow my head and try again, making it this time: *Vaad ha-Lashon*.

interested in the language as Finnish is one of Hungarian's few linguistic relatives in Europe. While a great many primitive words (fish, bird, hand, foot, one, two, three, etc.) and also some basic and peculiar grammatical rules are the same in both languages, I could not really understand one single word of Finnish. But I could recognize Finnish without fail: the intonation of both languages is the same, Finnish sounds like Hungarian, Hungarian sounds like Finnish. Both languages always stress the first syllable of the word and the voice drops at the end of each sentence; thus these languages have a regular, monotonous sound, like the beating of a drum. Following my own rule, I had never failed to recognize Finnish. Any language sounding like Hungarian which I couldn't understand was bound to be Finnish. Now, Hungarians are reputed to speak atrocious Hebrew – worse than any other nationality. Perhaps this is because in Hebrew people emphasize the final syllables of words and raise their voices at the end of a sentence – rules all Hungarian speakers disregard with pride and disdain. This habit, however, spoilt my old rule. Today I know that someone talking what sounds like Hungarian but isn't is not necessarily a Finn. He could also be a Hungarian speaking Hebrew.

The relationship between Hebrew and Yiddish has also changed in the last twenty years. Yiddish used to be more frowned upon – almost persecuted – in Israel than it was in Poland or pre-Hitler Germany. Yiddish was a bastard language, slightly comical, the tongue of the funny Jew as the anti-semite saw him. Israelis felt that Yiddish had nothing to do with Israel. But Polish and other Central European Jews – in some respects the most exasperating creatures, in others the cream of the nation – felt that Yiddish, whatever anti-semites might think, was a part of Jewish tradition and, indeed, remembering certain chapters of Jewish history and some writers who had written in Yiddish, a very notable part of that tradition. These people strongly objected to the oppression of Yiddish which they regarded as an anti-semitic trend in Israel. In addition, they, in turn, objected to Hebrew as Israel's national language. Hebrew was the Language of the Book, they said, and it was sacrilege to use it as the language of the marketplace and of the bedroom. By today Yiddish has seen a splendid revival, thanks mostly to the brilliant achievement of a Yiddish Theatre. No one objects to Yiddish any longer; no one is hostile. Hebrew has grown strong enough to be kind and tolerant to Yiddish.

*　　*　　*

I met some old friends in Haifa who had recently arrived from Transylvania and found Hebrew even more difficult than most Hungarians. They made noble efforts to cope with it but had to concede defeat. One day I went down to do some shopping with the lady of the house and watched a little Arab boy – about fifteen – serving his customers and talking to them in fluent and, as it seemed to me, idiomatic and accentless Hebrew. (Arabs are superb linguists.) When our turn came, my friend and the Arab boy spoke English.

'But he speaks Hebrew,' I told her.

She blushed.

'*He* does. But I don't.'

How to Avoid Food

Israel, on the whole, is one of the most exciting and exhilarating places in the world today: she keeps changing and she is struggling – most successfully – against overwhelming odds. Israel is a brave little country, looking to the future, and she can teach the whole of humanity a lesson or two. Also, Israel is *different*. It is possible to travel from New York to Singapore or from Sydney to Johannesburg and – unless you keep your eyes very much open – not notice that you have moved at all, but this will not be true if you take in Israel. Many travellers have gone round the world seeing nothing but the lobbies of Hilton Hotels, with the same American faces waiting to be taken on guided tours and, while waiting, drinking the same undrinkable American coffee of which the whole American nation is so inordinately proud. In Israel even Hilton-travellers notice a change because the Tel-Aviv Hilton differs from all other Hiltons. In all the other places I know I hated these institutions; I only moderately disliked the one in Tel-Aviv. (And the *gefillte fisch*, one of the glories of Polish-Jewish cuisine, is the best any Hilton serves anywhere – if they *do* serve it elsewhere – and very good indeed in its own right.)

Having said all this and having said earlier that people whose main interest in life is night clubs and striptease shows would do well to avoid Israel, I have to add: those people who are interested only and exclusively in the delights of gastronomy should visit France before (or instead of) going to Israel.

You can eat well in Israel if you are prepared to pay a lot. Among the very expensive restaurants there are some which are really excellent – perhaps not world-beaters, but even the most spoilt client will approve of them. It is in the medium price-bracket that Israel fails: there are no restaurants as far as I know (and as far as many Israeli friends know) where you can get a really good meal at a medium price. Anyone who supplies this need in Tel-Aviv will grow rich. I thought of trying my hand at it myself: restaurants have always fascinated me with the endless variety of people who come and go, and with their secrets and intrigues, carefully hidden in the kitchen and the pantries. But on second thoughts I asked myself: would it really be wise, after a lifelong experience in writing and journalism, to go and open a medium-price restaurant in Tel-Aviv, however badly it is needed? I got cold feet, I confess. So somebody else will grow rich instead of me – it has happened before.

When you reach the lower price level, you may be luckier again. Some of the dairy restaurants serve cold, fresh and delicious dairy products. Here, as in so many aspects of Israeli life, you are again reminded of the conflict between East and West. More of this problem of Eastern Jews and Arab Jews in the next chapter; here I only want to say that almost all of the good, cheap restaurants are run by Yemeni, Iraqi and other Arab Jews.

Genuine Arab restaurants – in East Jerusalem and on the West Bank – have also become deservedly popular. Arab food is more suitable for the climate than those famous and often excellent dishes developed in the snows of Poland and Russia; but few people believe this and, when I taste good Jewish dishes in Israel, I am glad they don't. Nevertheless, while Arab food is delicious, the best Arab restaurants are not any cheaper than the best Jewish ones. The waiters have a disconcerting habit of listening to your orders with great patience and courtesy, and then bringing you three times as much as you have ordered. When, somewhat timidly, you point this out, they take half of the surplus away with a hurt look in their eyes. In some Arab places you order beef and they bring you lamb; you order veal and they bring you lamb; you order pork and they bring you lamb. An obvious stratagem may have occurred to you – but it is no use: you order lamb with an *arrière pensée* and they will bring you lamb.

53

You leave the centre of Tel-Aviv and a few hundred yards
from the Mograbi you are in the Yemenite quarter: you have
left Europe and have reached the Middle East. It is, however,
an improved version of the Middle East. People do live in the
street and their dominant language is Arabic; they may be
squatting around or leaning in doorways with more or less
inscrutable faces (after working hours, that is, because during
the day, they work); and there are more potato peelings and
fruit stones thrown away on the pavement than are required to
make the place picturesque. But it is all much cleaner than the
corresponding type of street would be in the Middle East
proper: it looks healthier; you know that it is absolutely safe
to buy everything displayed in the windows of butcher-shops,
partly because these people have learnt a lot in Israel and partly
because the authorities are merciless in questions of hygiene.
In any case, the best cheap restaurants of Tel-Aviv are in this
district. A few have become chi-chi and cater for tourists but
a few others have kept their character and they are, to my
taste, the best eating places in the country – and that includes
the expensive places, too.

Yet, when you take up the menu in one of these excellent
little places and find such items as *Filled Sea Fish on Fire*, or
Roast Fish in Extent, you wonder. When you are offered *Eggs of
Adult Ox in Extent*, you are convinced – for a fleeting moment –
that Nasser must have something to do with this. But when you
return to the European parts of Tel-Aviv, go into one of the
horrible little restaurants there and get a bony, dry and
smelly piece of chicken for your lunch – don't you just long for
a good Egg of Adult Ox – and In Extent, at that!

Politics

Israel is trying hard to solve two basic political problems. There are, of course, many other issues discussed and debated, but almost all of these are either local, parochial or short-term. One of the two outstanding issues is a problem created by success: what to do with the occupied territories. The other was created by failure: the failure of the largest Israeli party to obtain an absolute majority. This problem is – how to diminish the obnoxious political influence of the religious zealots?

Israel is a democracy. Her Parliament – the Knesset – is elected on a basis of proportional representation. This electoral system is the enemy of the two-party system and always produces too many political parties. Israeli parties had the unfortunate further tendency to multiply by self-duplication: every major quarrel produced a split and quite a few splinter groups and factions formed new parties until even the Israelis decided that enough was enough. So nowadays there is a reversal of this tendency and, whenever possible, the parties and splinter groups form larger units. Three parties of the Left, Mapai (the original Israeli Labour Party), Achdut Ha'avoda (a pioneering Zionist group, particularly strong in the communal settlements) and Rafi (an influential splinter group, originally with Ben Gurion as its moving spirit) have formed the United Israel Labour Party; on the Right, the Gahal is a coalition of the Israel Liberal Party and the extreme nationalist Herut. The creation of the new United Israel Labour Party was necessitated not only for political but also for personal reasons. Mr Levi Eshkol, the Prime Minister, belongs to Mapai, the main party in the coalition, but Mr Eshkol's likeliest successors belong to two smaller parties: Mr Igal Allon to the Achdut Ha'avoda and General Moshe Dayan to Rafi.[1] Now both the Premier and the two pretenders are members of the United Israel Labour Party.

The country has always been governed by a coalition but today it is governed by a so-called Grand Coalition which is a more polite word for all and sundry. This Grand Coalition was founded in an hour of great national emergency: on June 5, 1967, on the first day of the Six Day War. National unity was of overwhelming importance and the formation of this Grand Coalition cannot but remind us of the great days of the Conservative-Labour coalition in Britain during the Second World War. What was right and significant in time of war, has become almost meaningless in the days of so-called peace, or at least of truce; yet the keeping together of this meaningless coalition, to preserve the unity of the non-united is – as we shall see presently – one of the main tactical aims of the Government.

The Opposition is infinitesimal: 108 members out of 120 support the Government. Three of the twelve opposition members are Communists, split among themselves and representing two hostile groups. One Communist Party, the Rakah, follows the Moscow line, stigmatizes Israel as aggressor and demands immediate withdrawal from the occupied territories. This party might remind one of the pro-Nazi Jews of Germany in 1933, who were alleged to demonstrate *for* Hitler, carrying legends: '*Heil Hitler, hinaus mit uns!*' ('Heil Hitler, Out With Us!') but the two cases are in fact different. The Rakah is largely a pro-Arab party, and quite a few of its communist members are not communists at all but Arab nationalists disguised as communists. (So when they shout '*Hinaus mit uns!*' – 'Out with us from the Occupied Territories' – they make better sense than the Jews of Germany did in 1933.) The other Communist Party, the Maki, under the leadership of Dr Moshe Sneh, faced the

[1] Mr Eshkol died on February 26, 1969, and was replaced by Mrs Golda Meir. But as at the time of my visit (summer, 1968) he was the Prime Minister I leave references to him unchanged.

57

realities of the situation. After June 1967 one could not be both a Muscovite Communist *and* an Israeli. It was either – or. The Maki is still faithful to communist ideals but has broken with Moscow (like so many other communist parties) and on this particular issue its line is: 'No withdrawal without peace.'

The great political debate turns, as I have already mentioned, on this question of withdrawal. Talking about it, you gain the impression that Israel's, say, two million politically conscious citizens have two million and one different plans to solve the problem. This, however, is not so; the various views are much nearer to one another than they seem at first sight. Some people start off from the extreme nationalistic point of view and declare: 'What we have conquered we have conquered with the blood of our sons, and it is ours. What we hold we keep. Not a square inch back!' The other extreme is not only anti-nationalist but also anti-Zionist. Israel, they maintain, must cease being a Zionist state and must become part of the Middle East where she belongs. Israel must become a bilingual, Jewish-Arab state in the Middle East – after all she has much more to do with Palestine Arabs than with New York Jews. In a re-united Jewish-Arab Palestine the question of what to do with these territories would lose its significance.

These opposite views seem irreconcilable; in fact, they are almost identical. The extreme right wing – after brief discussion and letting off some steam – will agree that Israel should make considerable sacrifices in order to achieve *real peace* (in other words: the 'not-a-square-inch-back' theory would become 'quite a lot of square-inches back'). The other extreme will agree that while their aims are the only right ones in the long run, for the time being it is not practicable to speak of Israel as becoming part of the Middle East, since the rest of the Middle East has only one ardent desire: that Israel should not be part of it.

Scratch the Israelis, have serious discussions with them, and you will find that once the slogans have been shouted and the dust has settled, ninety-nine out of a hundred will agree on these points:

(a) Jerusalem has become part of Israel, it has been incorporated and it will never be given up. Jerusalem is not negotiable.
Why this should be so is not quite clear to me. I know that most
Israelis feel extremely strongly about Jerusalem, but feeling –
however passionate – is not argument. They say, rightly,
that Jerusalem is a holy city of Judaism, but it is also a holy
city of Islam and Christendom. They add that Jerusalem is
an ancient Jewish city which has almost always had a Jewish
majority throughout its history, which is true: no one will deny
that Israel has a strong claim to Jerusalem. To divide the city
again would be madness and Israel has probably a stronger
claim to undivided Jerusalem than has Jordan. One solution
would be for the holy places to be put under international
control, and Jerusalem might become a capital city containing
an independent 'city', as Rome contains the Vatican. There
are many other possible solutions, but in any case the fate of
Jerusalem must be decided at the conference table in con-
junction with other problems. The fact that both Arabs and
Jews have always wanted to raise the problems which suited
them but not the other side; that both have constantly declared
one issue or another 'not negotiable', has plagued Arab-Israeli
relations ever since the War of Independence of 1948 and
landed us in the mess in which we find ourselves today.

(b) The Golan Heights cannot be returned, they say, because
they represent a dagger in Israel's heart. (During the winter of
1966–7 there was almost daily shelling of settlements, and life
in the Galilee became extremely difficult.) There are no Arabs
left in Golan in any case – they all fled in June 1967, only
6,000 friendly Druses stayed behind who prefer to live under
Israeli rule.

(c) Gaza is, in a sense, a southern Golan, i.e. a southern
dagger. It was always part of Palestine and was never
incorporated into Egypt, so it could not be 'given back' to
Egypt. The Gaza strip is too near to Tel-Aviv to be left in
hostile hands. Nevertheless, all the problems of refugees, possible
compensation, etc. should be negotiated.

(d) The Sinai Peninsula must be abandoned sooner or later,
and Egypt – the Israelis feel – should make great concessions

59

to get back her oil wells and to be able to re-open the Suez Canal, provided Israeli ships can use it too. Israel does not want to keep these territories but evacuation must be discussed in the framework of a general settlement.

(e) That leaves us with the West Bank of the Jordan. It is this territory that is the real bone of contention. Some supporters of the *Eretz Israel* Movement (i.e. the 'not-a-square-inch-back' crowd) want to keep everything, because they regard Israel as the natural heir of Palestine; others are prepared to return almost everything (but even they would insist on frontier rectifications near Latrun where Israel was only eight miles broad) – but only if and when a proper peace treaty is signed; others again would like to see the West Bank turned into an independent Palestinian Arab state. But many others oppose this plan on the grounds that such a state would inevitably become an Israeli satellite, and a satellite state is a nuisance for everyone. Such a state would provoke furious Arab hostility and instead of becoming a bridge between Jews and Arabs would become a new, highly explosive issue. On this point, the political left and right overlap: one might expect the right to want to retain territories while the left would be more conciliatory. This is a mistake. The right wing want to see a Jewish nationalist state and are not at all keen on a million extra Arab citizens and voters. It is the left who are prepared to accept them. And it is, indeed, the hope of some moderate *Arab* nationalists that Israel will incorporate the West Bank because this way, they think, the West Bank Arabs plus the original Israeli Arabs (who stayed in Israel in 1948) would gain a majority in a few decades and Palestine would thus be reconquered without firing a shot.

There are further – indeed innumerable – variations on this theme. One often hears that the Israelis would genuinely like to have peace; but as the Arabs are obviously and indeed openly preparing for a fourth round, Israel might as well hold on to the occupied territories and start that fourth round from strategically more advantageous positions. It is a feature of the problem that both sides are ready to 'solve' those issues which interest them while leaving the inconvenient problems unsolved. Arabs insist on withdrawal and on the resettlement of the refugees; Israelis on a peace treaty. It seems reasonable that the problem should be considered *in toto* and not piecemeal – a peace conference may break up, but piecemeal negotiations are doomed to failure even before they start.

Israel's insistence on a peace treaty is sometimes described as naïve. A peace treaty, it is said, is simply a scrap of paper which the Arabs – particularly if encouraged by the Russians – could tear up at any moment. But while history teaches us that a peace treaty is no absolute guarantee of peace – and while, indeed, even the most optimistic of the pro-Arab Israelis know that they could put no unrestricted faith in the signatures of Arab leaders – yet it would still be an advance if the Arabs sat down to negotiate with the Israelis after saying on so many occasions that they would not do so, and if they signed a treaty, thus recognizing Israel's existence and giving her *frontiers* instead of the *military front* or *armistice line* which she has had to be content with since 1948 – frontiers which would, in turn, limit her expansion.

The trouble is that it would be a terribly bitter pill for any Arab leader to swallow, and perhaps not only a bitter pill but political suicide, a downright impossibility for any leader who wishes to remain in power. The Arabs have talked themselves into a situation from which they cannot escape. They have always vied with each other to show that he who is most anti-Israel is the best Arab patriot. Hatred of Israel has been the only issue in recent years on which they could agree, and any Arab leader who dared utter a reasonable or conciliatory word would be swept away by his own people. Or if his own people didn't rise spontaneously, other Arab leaders would see to it that they rose, like it or not. Nasser, for instance, sometimes gives the impression of being fed up with the Israeli problem and wishing that he could concentrate on other issues in order to regain his lost position in the Arab world and the world at large. He cannot do so. He is the prisoner of his own collected speeches. However ready he may be to say that three defeats are enough for the time being and that some at least temporary accommodation should be made with Israel, this is a luxury he

61

cannot afford. Years ago the Syrians called him a traitor because they thought he was soft with Israel. He cannot risk this again. To remain in power after losing the war was miraculous enough. But he knows that deeds count for less in the Arab world than words: he can afford to lose wars but he certainly cannot afford to be less flamboyant. Strategy is less important than rhetoric.

* * *

I have been referring so far to the attitudes of people – official and unofficial – to whom I spoke in Israel. But what is the attitude of the Israeli Government? This is – as our American brethren say – the 64,000 dollar question. The Israeli Government is silent. Well, no Israeli is ever silent; in this case, too, 'silent' means that they have talked too much. Various members of the Grand Coalition have spoken in so many voices and put forward so many diametrically opposed views that for a while supreme confusion reigned. Ministers were often forced to declare that they had been speaking in their own names and not as members of the Government – which was absurd and pitiful. Eventually the Prime Minister forbade his erratic and loquacious crew to utter any further views on this subject and made it clear that only he himself and his Foreign Minister were entitled to pronounce on these issues. After this stern warning Mr Eshkol and Mr Eban remained silent and the others – who were forbidden to speak and did not count in any case – went on talking in whispers.

The Israeli Government has good reasons for remaining silent on these matters.

Israel feels that she is unable to proclaim her peace aims before the other side has even agreed to sit down at the conference table. If Israel declared that she wanted to retain great chunks of Arab territories, the Arabs would have good reason for a public outcry, they would call attention to Israel's imperialistic designs and would, in all likelihood, withdraw from the negotiations. If, on the other hand, the Israelis declared the true limits of their concessions – if they were extremely conciliatory – they would lose all their bargaining power. They would have to start negotiating from the weakest position. Refusal to make further concessions would show them up as stubborn and rigid, while if they gave a true indication of their maximum concessions, further concessions would be impossible. Israel – there is almost general agreement on this – cannot put all her cards on the table before the other side declares that he is ready to play cards at all. First sit down, then we talk, they say.

Very well, say quite a few critics of the Government. Do not declare your intentions publicly, but at least clarify them for yourselves. State publicly that you, yourselves, know what you intend to do. But the Israeli Government cannot make such a declaration. The reason for this is simple: they have no idea what they want to do. Detailed discussions on this issue would blow up the Government and end the coalition. All politicians know that such a wide coalition is unrealistic in peace-time; that it cannot last too long. Yet, it holds for the time being. And why should they create, almost artificially, a major political crisis, just to be ready for negotiations which may never come? Why create a real and immediate crisis for the sake of a possible but improbable and in any case remote peace conference?

Both sides believe that time is on their side. But continuous border incidents – retaliatory raids and the aerial bombardment of Salt, near Amman, in August; a serious bomb explosion in the Jewish part of Jerusalem in November 1968 and growing guerilla activities in 1969 – show that time works for neither; it is against both. Time makes both sides more intransigent. And a little more intransigence is not exactly the greatest need in the Israeli-Arab dispute.

RELIGIOUS PRESSURE

The political power of Orthodox Jews is an old plague of Israel. Ten years ago – when the capital was still divided – I was driving along in Jerusalem. We had left the elegant and clean streets of the centre and were driving through rather dirty parts, full of people in long, black kaftans with round hats and side whiskers and, as a rule, a sullen and hostile look on their faces. A lady in the car, struck by this sudden change of environment, looked around uneasily and then, having solved the mystery, exlaimed: 'I see . . . We are in the Jewish quarter of Jerusalem.'

She was right. That was exactly where we were. To understand the situation we must remember the role of Orthodox Jews, mostly of Russian and Polish origin, in Israeli society. These Polish Jews are in a sense the best element in Jewry: they are devoted to their religion, they are brave, they are unbending. They faced inhuman persecution for centuries but stuck to the faith of their fathers. They were spat upon, laughed at, exploited and many of them were murdered, yet they went on doing what they regarded as right; they went on serving a God who showed little love and tenderness for them. Their suffering made them strong and noble; it also made them bigoted, intolerant and self-righteous.

When they arrived in Israel, they could not change their attitudes from one day to the next. They were used to persecution; they had thrived on persecution; they needed persecution. It was a challenge which had always made them respond in magnificent fashion, from the times of the Pharaohs to the days of the Warsaw Ghetto. So they needed anti-semitism even in Israel, and what they needed, they got.

It seems that every nation – every group of people – needs Jews on whom to unload a certain amount of nastiness and the baser sort of aggression; and the Jews were chosen for this role centuries ago because the Jews were extremely suitable for the role of Jews. But this need to persecute a minority is alive also in the heart of the Jews themselves, simply because they are neither better nor worse than other people. They are people themselves (a theory the world has refused to accept for many centuries). The modern, hard-working, Europeanized, anti-religious Israelis were irritated by these pale, unathletic people, busy reading and explaining the Talmud and doing nothing else, and looking as if they had just escaped from the pages of the *Stuermer*. It was unfair to be irritated, but the Jewish anti-semites, like all the others, rationalized and streamlined their irritation to suit their purpose. Their line was that the zealots were not pulling their weight, were taking out from the community more than they contributed to it, that they were shirking

military service, etc. In fact, many of the Orthodox Jews *are* pulling their weight. Religious studies are, after all, recognized in all civilized states as legitimate pursuits; and many Orthodox Jews are, in any case, doing a lot more than just reading the Talmud: they are engaged in business, industry and in the various professions; and while a number try to avoid military service, many others serve in the army. (Many of those who refuse do so on grounds of conviction: they do not recognize the Zionist state. Zionists should not have founded the Jewish state; this was a task to be left to the Messiah. This view – like many others held by these zealots – enrages modern Israelis.) But what about tolerance? It is easy to be tolerant on issues one does not feel strongly about. All the Jews, quite rightly, claimed tolerance for themselves throughout the ages. Why not grant it to fellow Jews?

The trouble begins when these people are not satisfied with religious freedom but insist on political power as well. The political constellation under Ben Gurion – as well as Ben Gurion's concentration on other and more important issues – favoured them. In various coalitions Mapai needed the support of the religious parties; with them it had a majority in Parliament. Their support had to be bought by concessions. On top of it all, many American Jews who gave a lot of money to Israel insisted on seeing Israel as a devout, religious state. Many of these Americans were not too religious themselves; but they felt Israel ought to be. The result of all this is that Israel became in one respect a backward country. There is no civil marriage in Israel, a Jew cannot marry a non-Jew; a Cohenite cannot marry a divorced woman (a Supreme Court judge had to go and marry in America, i.e. to break the law); all matrimonial jurisdiction is in the hands of the Rabbinical Courts, who act in a spirit which was outdated at the time of Jesus; only kosher – and consequently dearer – meat is readily available; the Jewish Sabbath, bringing public transport to a standstill almost everywhere, makes the Scottish Sunday look positively frivolous. The zealots say that it is outrageous to be disturbed by the noise of sabbath-breaking motor-cars and buses on the way to the synagogue; they find nothing outrageous in depriving the great majority of the population of their chosen way of life. The zealots claim they act in God's name and God, alas, can never protest against iniquities and injustices committed in his name. In Israel it may be your honest and firm conviction that God does not exist and that the Sabbath is for enjoyment and recreation. But such views are branded as sinful and immoral and fifteen per cent of the population is permitted to terrorize the rest, or at least to impose a way of life on them which they resent and detest.

The political situation is slowly changing and the *Mizrachi* – the zealots – are losing ground. But even if they cannot gain new concessions, no political party dares to touch the old system and bring a hornet's nest about its ears. So the outdated marriage laws remain and the Saturday Observance Society, so to say, goes on reigning supreme.

The objection to this religious bullying is twofold. Jewish clericalism and bigotry are no more likeable or tolerable than Catholic, Lutheran or Shintoist clericalism and bigotry; or Communist and anti-Communist bigotry for that matter. Secondly, to claim that it is part of the Jewish Way of Life is a dangerous argument. Israel was founded to give persecuted Jews a refuge and a homeland, to give them a chance to live like other nations. It was not founded to create an outlet for Jewish clerical intolerance and bigotry. To legalize the superiority of Judaism over other religions and not to allow Jews to marry Christians is a step towards establishing a new South Africa. This phrase, 'new South Africa', is, incidentally, not mine; I am quoting a clear-sighted, moderate and not even anti-religious Israeli professor. 'We don't want to become a master-race,' he added. 'We have been the chosen people long enough. God should now choose another one.'

There is a difference between a *Jewish state* and a *purely Jewish state*. A Jewish state is a necessary and welcome addition to our modern world; a purely Jewish state is the first step on a slippery slope.

*   *   *

Curiously, both problems, the problem of the occupied territories and the problem of clerical pressure, are the same
problem. In the first case, national intolerance, in the second
religious intolerance must come to terms with the demands of
a modern world. One feels in Israel that to come to terms with
Arab nationalism will not be any more difficult than to come
to terms with religious zealots. In fact, listen to some of the
zealots and you come to the conclusion that Nasser, Hussein
and even the Syrians represent sweet reasonableness compared
with the rabbis.

A Racial Problem

When Israel was established, and even in the preceding years, the country was full of professional people who had found their university degrees useless in their country of origin and found them equally useless in Israel. In Europe, in many cases, they were not allowed to practise their professions because they were Jews; and in Israel they no longer wanted to practise them. Israel needed peasants, electricians, bricklayers and navvies, she had more than enough barristers, heart-specialists, chartered accountants and doctors of *classica philologia*. 'The legend runs,' I wrote in my earlier book, 'that when Nathanya – a German settlement north of Tel-Aviv – was being built, a visitor saw a long line of people passing bricks to one another and heard, at the same time, a strange murmur. Coming nearer he was able to catch the words. As each member of the line received and passed on a brick he said: "*Danke Herr Doktor, bitte Herr Doktor, danke Herr Doktor, bitte Herr Doktor*".'

This '*Danke Herr Doktor*' era was ended by the influx of Arabic Jews, which started with the Yemenites, in 1947. The Yemen, the most backward of all the Arabic states, contained a large Jewish population. Their ancestors moved to Yemen forty-two years before the destruction of the First Temple (586 BC). In 1947 they heard about the establishment of the new Jewish State, passed through the Arabian desert on foot and were flown from Aden to Lydda ('Operation Magic Carpet'). They were religious and as poor and ignorant as the poorest Arab fellahin – but they were intelligent and quick at learning. They acted as porters and carriers as far as their fragile physique permitted, they opened bazaars and carried on as small traders. They were clannish, loyal to one another, formed a political party and became less and less religious: in Israel, they felt, religion was no longer necessary.

Many other Arabic Jews followed: from Egypt, Iraq and North Africa, where (except in Morocco) they were persecuted to varying degrees. The Arab governments occasionally declared that while they had nothing against Jews – they doted on Jews – they were deadly enemies of the Zionists. They forgot to add that, as far as they were concerned, a Jew was a Zionist and a Zionist was a Jew. In many Arab lands there is discriminatory legislation against the Jews and further discrimination is practised without legal basis. Nasser admitted that his sympathies during World War II had been with the Germans, and he often referred to the *Protocols of the Elders of Zion* as an important, valid and revealing document. Moslem Arabs posed as staunch champions of Christianity and declared that the Jews had to pay for the crucifixion of Christ. When the Pope changed his mind on this and exonerated the Jews, Moslem Arabs attacked the Pope for having failed in his Christian duties. The result of Arab propaganda and persecution was that a tremendous number of poor, badly educated and often illiterate Jews arrived in Israel. They came whenever they could leave the Arab lands. By 1966 just under one third of Israel's population was born in Asia and Africa but to these one has to add a considerable number of Eastern Jews born in Israel. As far as the ethnic face of the population is concerned, Israel is losing a great deal of her European character and according to statisticians Eastern Jews will soon form the majority.

Initially, this threat – if threat it is – posed a racial problem. The fifties – particularly the mid-fifties – was a bad period for Israel. Although living conditions had improved, there was disillusionment in the air, the pioneering spirit seemed to be dying out, many Israelis were departing for quieter and safer lands (a number of them seemed to come to Israel only to obtain a passport) and the country was uneasy and unhappy. On top of it all, the influx of the dark-skinned Arabic Jews was creating a highly embarrassing racial problem for Israel. This era of depression passed after five years or so: morale rose, a great deal of the earlier enthusiasm returned. The change was due to many factors but one might as well remark here that two men did more for Israel than anyone else. These two are not President Weizmann and Ben Gurion; they are Adolf Hitler and Nasser. No one says that their contribution was not involuntary, still less that they deserve any gratitude. Yet, the fact remains that but for Hitler's horrible crimes Israel would not exist today; but for Nasser's (and his predecessor's) folly and blunders Israel would be a tiny, struggling, hardly viable country within the borders designated by the 1948 United Nations' partition plan.

But, as I have said, the racial clash lingered on the horizon in the fifties. The Eastern Jews complained that they were treated as second class citizens; that they were given menial jobs and could not get on in the army; that intermarriages were rare; that they were the victims of apartheid.

The European Jews tried to hush up this subject: it smelt of racialism and was most embarrassing. The influx of the Easterners – as many people saw it – threatened to turn Israel into just another Middle Eastern state with a poor, uneducated and backward population. They also feared that the morale of the army was bound to suffer if too many of its soldiers were Eastern Jews.

The truth is that Eastern Jews were discriminated against socially but not on a racial basis. The gap between rich and poor and, more important, between educated and uneducated, could not be closed overnight; not even if all concerned happened to be Jews. Eastern Jews were mostly privates in the army and only few of them rose to the high rank of a corporal; but illiterates could not be appointed Lieutenant-Generals. This went for jobs, too: unskilled workers have to carry loads, peel potatoes, sweep the streets and do other simple jobs and cannot be appointed managing directors of vast corporations. All these are facts of life; but another painful and disturbing fact was that a racial cleavage seemed more and more apparent.

Time passed. Many of the immigrants got some education and of course not all of them had been illiterate or even poorly educated to start with. But *opportunity* was not barred to them:

schools and other facilities were open; no one was turned down for a job because he had come from Tunis or Iraq; no one was refused entry to the university because he had come from Tripoli instead of Vienna. The gap narrowed but it did not disappear. In a gang of navvies you still find more Arabic than European faces; on the general staff European faces only. There is a difference in the standard of living: the average Easterner lives on a lower standard than the average Westerner. The army, however, is a great leveller: all, male and female citizens, do military service and the common experience of years leaves its mark.

The effect of the Six Day War was most beneficial in this respect. The Eastern Jews, far from lowering morale, proved themselves brave and devoted soldiers. Their record is impeccable and their prestige rose. I heard their praises sung so often and so emphatically that I gained the firm impression that the Eastern Jews have at last arrived in Israel. And – which must make this fact even more satisfactory to them – they have arrived by their own exertions.

The war had another effect. With the occupied territories, almost another million Arabs came under Israeli administration. Arabic became an even more important language than before and a knowledge of Arabic a great asset. As all Eastern Jews speak Arabic, many thus benefited. Equally important: the Eastern Jews – certainly the older ones – are, in fact, Arab in habits, outlook and way of thinking. An Israeli Arab, a very loyal and trusted citizen, told me: 'The division in this country is not between Jew and Arab; it is between Easterners and Europeans.'

This is partly oversimplification, partly wishful thinking on his part. Yet, it contained more than a grain of truth. If an old Iraqi or Moroccan Jew goes into an Arab house on the West Bank he feels at home. He smokes the *narghile* with his Arab host, and if he meets an Arab from Baghdad or Casablanca he will have more in common with him than with a Jew from Leeds, Warsaw or San Francisco. When an Arab remarks to an Eastern Jew (as one remarked to me), speaking of mini-skirts: 'My mother used to hide her face even from close

relations, but my daughter displays her thighs to all and sundry – what is the world coming to?' the remark will not sound the same as it did to me or would to any Israeli of European descent, but will be recognized by an Arab Jew as a heartfelt cry which he understands, shares and sympathizes with.

The East-West gap is slowly, very slowly, narrowing. Inter-marriages occur but are still far from frequent. If a European Jew appears at a party with a Yemenite girl, for example, the couple will be received kindly, but after they have left will become a 'case' to be discussed and commented upon.

Will the Eastern Jews turn Israel into a Middle Eastern state? The fashionable answer is: yes, if Israel is lucky. People keep insisting that she *must* become a Middle Eastern state. A Mediterranean state, perhaps; but when the main aim of all Arabs, whatever they may say about Western Imperialism, is to become European, why should the only European state in the Middle East have to become Middle Eastern?

'But what about colour?' some Israelis ask in a whisper. 'Are we all going to be brown in fifty years time?' Now, it seems to me that becoming brown *would* be lucky. It's a very nice colour, and such a slight metamorphosis, if only it could happen to the whole of humanity, would rid us of the gravest problem – and such a pointless one, too – of our time, as well as making us look much better.

Names

I offended more people in Israel than anywhere else, ever in my life.

Someone rings you up and says 'This is Ephraim Bar'on speaking.'

'What can I do for you?' you ask politely if somewhat hesitantly.

Ephraim Bar'on bangs the receiver down and will never speak to you again because of your unforgivable pomposity, coolness and unfriendliness.

It turns out that the last time you were in Israel you and Ephraim Bar'on were bosom friends – but his name at that time was Marcel Brandeis. He changed it years ago, and it's true that he never notified you, but all the same you are supposed to have guessed that Ephraim Bar'on couldn't possibly be anyone else but your old pal Marcel Brandeis.

Sometimes there is a little traffic in the wrong direction. I was told about a Yemenite whose name was Elijahu Yehuda – a Hebrew name to dream about, with its famous connotations. But he disliked this name intensely. He had never heard of the great Ben Yehuda, and besides, now he was in Israel he wanted a nice *Jewish* name as he understood a Jewish name. So he changed to Schmuel Goldstein and has lived happily ever after.

After one or two bad experiences with changed names you start asking, tentatively and politely, what your caller's name used to be. This is regarded as rude. Israelis, with rare exceptions such as Mr Elijahu Yehuda, are trying to get away from all the German-sounding Jewish names, and no one wants to be reminded that once, in Slovakia or Montenegro, he carried such a name instead of the long, melodious and beautiful Hebrew one he has now. And Christian – or rather first – names are just as difficult. Your old friend Peter is now Akiba, Joe is Igal, Steve is Aharon. The Bible has been ransacked for names still unused, and now, with the single exception of Cain, there is not one left.

You are on your own. It would be both very rude and heartless if you didn't know that Igal Gilboa is your childhood friend Pista Barna, from Budapest. *How* are you to know it? That is a problem you will have to solve for yourself.

A reference book entitled *Who Was Who* would be a most popular and useful publication in Israel today.

2 THE EMPIRE

How to be an Aggressor

In February 1964 President Nasser stated Egypt's policy:

'The possibilities of the future are war with Israel. It is we who will dictate the time. It is we who will dictate the place.'

He was as good as his word: he did dictate the time; he did dictate the place.

General Abdulla Ziad, the Syrian Defence Minister, declared in the same year:

'The Syrian Army stands as a mountain to crush Israel and demolish her. This Army knows how to crush its enemies.'

On May 25, 1967, Cairo Radio announced:

'The Arab people are firmly resolved to wipe Israel off the map and to restore the honour of the Arabs in Palestine.'

On May 30, 1967, having signed the Defence Pact with King Hussein, Nasser explained the purpose of the pact:

'This deed will astound the world. Today they will know that the Arabs are ready for the fray. The hour of decision has arrived.'

On June 4, one day before the outbreak of hostilities, Nasser made a further statement on Cairo Radio, talking to Israel directly:

'We are facing you in the battle and are burning with desire for it to start, in order to obtain revenge. This will make the world realize what the Arabs are and what Israel is.'

Boasts and bloodthirsty threats of this type were poured out by Arab politicians, radios and newspapers, day and night for twenty years. There are several hundred quotations in front of me – and even those are only a tiny fraction of the horrifying total. I am going to quote a few more because I feel the reader really ought to inhale the spirit of these utterances and familiarize himself with the beauty of their style and the nobility of their inspiration:

'This will be a momentous war of extermination which will be spoken of in history like the Mongolian massacres and the Crusades.' (Azzem Pasha, Secretary General of the Arab League, before the Arabs were beaten in 1948.)

'In demanding the restoration of the refugees to Palestine, the Arabs intend that they shall return as masters of the homeland, not as slaves. More explicitly, they intend to annihilate the state of Israel.' (Mohammed Salah od Din, Egyptian Foreign Minister, October, 1949.)

'We want a decisive battle in order to annihilate that germ, Israel. All the Arabs want a decisive battle.' (Nasser in 1955.)

'If the Arabs return to Israel, Israel will cease to exist.' (Nasser in 1961.)

'. . . the riff-raff of mankind, a criminal gang surrounded by ninety million Arabs eager to trample upon it and wipe it out, a black colony – the right moment is sure to come when it will be possible to extirpate it [Israel] from the world.' (*Al Gomhouriya*, Cairo daily paper, April, 1961.)

I am getting tired of this and so, no doubt, is the reader. So only two further quotes. One from Ahmed Shukeiry, head of the Palestine Liberation Organization, the loudest-mouthed braggart of all, who a day or two before the outbreak of the Six Day War invited his friends and some Arab correspondents to have coffee with him on the Tel-Aviv sea-front but failed to keep the appointment. On May 16, he said:

'We are despatching the *fedayun* [his guerilla fighters] into the occupied land, one group after the other, so that they may annihilate the Israel gang. . . .'

The last quote comes from the *Voice of the Arabs* radio station. It said on May 17, 1967:

'Egypt with all her resources – human, economic and scientific – is prepared to plunge into a total war that will be the end of Israel.'

Today all this sounds more pathetic and comical than terrifying. The Syrian Army, that 'mountain, ready to crush Israel', ran away as fast as it could, abandoning one of the world's strongest lines of fortifications, rivalling the Maginot. Those other Arabs, 'burning with desire to fight', did not fight at all but fled, leaving behind the most modern Russian equipment – even huge, self-propelled guns, sometimes with the protecting canvas covers still on the barrels; the ninety million, so eager to plunge into total war, are whining now about Israel's *numerical superiority*.

This propaganda did not stop even after the war. Arab papers today write ironically: 'The Jews keep boasting about a Jewish victory and an Arab defeat' – as if the absurdity of the claim were self-evident. Immediately after the defeat (June 11, 1967) the following appeared in *El Ahram*:

'The war is believed by Israel to have been the last armed contest, but it was no more than a mere forerunner of a new war which is going to be more dangerous than any previous war, including that of 1967. This new war will be fought under the flag of the unity of all Arab forces, because the Arabs – at long last – have learnt their lessons from the past.'

The pre-war Arab boasts and threats were accompanied by even more explicit incitements to mass murder. The papers were full of cartoons showing the Jews as ugly, miserable cowards with hooked noses (the style borrowed from the *Stuermer*), about to be crushed, smashed, disembowelled by mighty and indomitable Arab heroes. Israel was a little worm about to be swallowed by a mighty Arab shark; Israel was the repulsive, old, hook-nosed peddler about to be kicked in the behind by the mighty boot of a glorious Arab warrior. (In the event, many of the glorious Arab warriors took off their mighty boots, so as to be able to run away faster in the Sinai Desert, and put a safe distance between themselves and the hook-nosed peddlers pursuing them.) A huge Arab hand was seen crushing a tiny cowardly Jewish soldier. Another cartoon showed three politicians – President Johnson, Harold Wilson and Levi Eshkol – climbing on one another's shoulders but even so failing to reach up to the belt of the mighty Arab soldier who was watching them with amused contempt. Four Arab guns were shown blowing a miserable *Stuermer*-Jew to smithereens; the victim, once again, was depicted as feeble, cowardly and repulsively ugly. There were innumerable scenes of Arabs hanging frightful Jews or executing them by other means; of brave Arab warriors disembowelling cowardly Israeli soldiers, anxiously watched by equally revolting-looking American bankers in top-hats; Arabs trampling on Jewish worms with their huge powerful feet.

But even in this campaign some help was needed. It was forthcoming. The Soviet Union has nothing to learn from the Arabs in the field of scurrilous obscenity. The Russians produced suitable stuff to encourage their allies and egg them on before leaving them in the lurch.

The cartoons in the Soviet newspapers were just as badly drawn, just as witless and – what is more important – just as incendiary and bloodthirsty as their Arab counterparts. They were clearly anti-semitic in the best Nazi tradition, with one extra embellishment: the Soviet cartoons actually accused the Jews of being the spiritual heirs of Hitler, their executioner. An ugly Jew, in one of these Russian cartoons, is shown bowing deeply and respectfully in front of a Nazi boot, practically licking it. Or take this quotation from *Sovietskaya Rossia*, published on May 21, 1967:

> 'From Tel-Aviv there pour announcements to the effect that Syria "is responsible" for the activities of the diversional groups allegedly operating from Syrian territory. *These groups are clearly mythical.*'

But months before (in January 1967) the Cairo press itself admitted, indeed claimed proudly, that the guerillas – who now became 'diversional groups' – did not operate 'allegedly', nor were they so clearly mythical:

'It appears that what is giving Israel sleepless nights and pushing her into repeated attacks on the Syrian border is her belief that Syria is encouraging the *fedayun* and the infiltrators. *Syria has not concealed this fact, nor has she denied it.*'

But if the entire Soviet press missed this announcement or did not recall it four months later, surely it ought to have remembered Shukeiry's above-quoted proud declaration *five days before the Soviet statement*, claiming that the Palestine Liberation Organization was despatching the *fedayun*, 'one group after the other', in order to 'annihilate the Israel gang.'

Arab threats were accompanied by warlike acts; in addition to the *fedayun* raids, the world witnessed the closing of the Straits of Tiran, the signing of the Defence Pact between Egypt and Jordan, later joined by Iraq ('the Arabs are ready for the fray') and the mobilisation of vast armies on Israel's frontiers.

'How to be an Aggressor' then? It is easy. If you do not wait patiently and with respectful timidity to be demolished; to be wiped off the map; to become the victim of Mongolian-style massacres; to be annihilated; liquidated; exterminated; to be crushed like a worm; to be hanged; to be shot to pieces and/or disembowelled by bayonets, then you become an aggressor.

Discussing these days, some British chroniclers have remarked: 'By this time the Israeli people had been whipped up into an extermination neurosis.'[1] A good phrase this: extermination neurosis. Some people, it is true, become a trifle nervous when they are about to be exterminated. And the Arabs, in many boastful pamphlets, trumpeted it abroad that they were not only determined but also perfectly able to do so. One Egyptian pamphlet assured its readers that Egypt alone could finish the job: Egypt had a population of 30.2 million, Israel only 2.6 million; Egypt had an enormous budget, Israel a miserably tiny one; Egypt produced 7.2 tons of petroleum annually while Israel produced none; Egypt produced 533,000 tons of

1 *Israel and Palestine*, by Bill Hillier. Housmans, London, 1968.

81

iron ore, Israel none; Egypt had nine medium-range missiles for every one Israeli, and Egypt also had long-range missiles while Israel had none. And so on – many other items were listed to show that Egypt alone could wipe Israel off the map. And on paper that was only too true.

The final Russo-Arab pretext was that Israel was about to attack Syria. When Eshkol, on receiving a Russian note of warning, informed the Russian Ambassador presenting it that there were no such plans and asked him to accompany him to the Syrian border, go wherever he pleased and see for himself that all was quiet there, that there were no Israeli troop-concentrations of any kind, the Ambassador replied that he was not concerned with facts and truth, he was only concerned with transmitting his Government's communications.

Israel may be criticized on many counts – and I too have said and am going to say what I feel about certain aspects of her policy. But even in the Gaza strip, when I asked a group of bitter, hostile, angry Arabs, full of implacable hatred for Israel: 'Who started the war?' they answered with a grin and without a moment's hesitation: 'Abdul Nasser.'

*   *   *

Russia's support of the Arabs was crucial, but in a sense the Russians are less of a problem than the Arabs. One of the many Russian traditions the world has grown used to is that during the rule of any one Big Brother, the least criticism of his most questionable views is tantamount to high treason. Then Big Brother number two comes along to tell us that his predecessor was a bungler, a criminal maniac, and an enemy of the people. It is true that Big Brother Number Two supported Big Brother Number One through thick and thin and in fact executed some of his bloodiest orders, but – well, *c'est la vie*, children, you know how it is. This new situation lasts until Big Brother Number Two is booted out and sent away to rot. At the moment of writing we have the Infallible Technocrat and the Infallible Bureaucrat for Big Brothers. No doubt they, too, will disappear from the stage one day and will be declared criminal imbeciles by their successors (who are at the moment serving them faithfully). This may happen too late to help Israel; but then again it may not.

The Arabs on the other hand, will not recover for a long time from the blow they suffered. Defeat produces – in many cases – a doctrine of racial superiority. This happened to some of the nations defeated by the Turks; it happened to the population of the American South defeated in the Civil War; it happened to the Germans after World War I; it happened to the Afrikaners, after their defeat in the Boer War. It seems to be happening now to the Arabs: they must, somehow, counterbalance their shame, otherwise it would be insupportable. If this feeling of superiority is in any way proportionate with the magnitude of their defeat, the Arabs are going to be the most superior people ever.

The Israelis – although modesty and tact is not one of their most conspicuous virtues – do not gloat over the Arab defeat and do not rub it in. That is all right and most commendable. But, at the same time, they let these threats, boasts and bloodthirsty prophecies fade from people's memory. They do not want to exasperate the Arabs. The Arabs are indeed a once great nation – with potentialities for a new era of greatness – and they have tremendous past achievements to their credit but today they live in a world of fantasy and fancy words; they share this with the Chinese, another once great nation now in decline, making a creditable (and occasionally very discreditable) effort to come back. Reluctance to gloat over your adversary's wounds and rub it in is one thing; but this clumsy reticence is quite another. To face reality, to stare it in the face at a moment of truth is a salutary experience which the Arabs must learn to bear. This preoccupation with 'saving face' and this pathological hatred of being laughed at does not deserve much respect and consideration. If you do not want to be laughed at, do not make yourself ridiculous.

*　　*　　*

What do the Arabs say about their war-mongering propaganda

today? Nothing. That is, nothing as long as they can afford to remain silent. If they are pressed hard they pooh-pooh the whole matter. It is another case of Jewish hysteria. The Arabs did not really mean anything quite so literally. Western people – to say nothing of the Jews – completely misunderstood Arab rhetoric. Arabs, they admit, are fond of expressing themselves a shade more colourfully than a *Times* leader, but that's all. A friend of mine met Nasser and put this question to him. Nasser was outraged. He said that he had children of his own and loved all children, and if anyone suggested that he really urged the indiscriminate murder of Jews of all ages and both sexes, he must be out of his mind. When the Arabs spoke of an apocalyptic war of extermination, and massacres which would dwarf the Mongolian blood-baths, they were speaking metaphorically. Poetically, really. But they never thought of actually harming little Jewish children and women. Whenever Nasser said 'Israel will cease to exist', he meant it politically. When Shukeiry declared that there would not be many survivors after the then impending war of 1967, all he had in mind was that U Thant ought to look into this matter again. At the headquarters of the Jordanian Hashemite Brigade, near Ramallah, the Israelis found some files, containing operational plans for raiding Israeli villages and settlements. One sentence reads: 'The intention of Headquarters Western Front is to carry out a raid on Motza colony, to destroy it and to kill all its inhabitants.'

Having read this, our diseased and suspicious Western minds are ready to jump to the conclusion that some of the inhabitants of Motza might have come to harm. Not at all. Arab soldiers, thus instructed, would have penetrated into Motza at night time armed with sub-machine-guns; but they would have been fully aware that the aim of their nocturnal raid was only to have the Palestine question raised once more in the General Assembly of the United Nations.

* * *

This Arab disclaimer was not put to the test because not one single Israeli village or settlement fell into Arab hands even for a few minutes. This, however, may not always be the case if there is a Fourth, Fifth and Sixth Round. They are afraid – those cowardly Jews – that twenty years of murder-propaganda may have made some effect on a few, not too highly educated, private soldiers who are not accustomed to reading poetry and who do not even know what a metaphor is.

The other explanation we hear is that the Arabs are not anti-semitic (how can they be, a Semitic race themselves?) but only anti-Zionist. Jews as a race they love; political Zionism they hate.

So if a few thousand throats had been cut owing to some regrettable misunderstanding, the owners of these throats could have rested assured that they were killed not as Jews but as Zionists.

A subtle distinction; but, from the point of view of international politics, an important one.

Warlike Interlude

'The Battle of Jerusalem was raging,' a friend of mine, a member of a tank crew, told me, 'and it was a stiff battle. For a few hours we encountered what was probably the stiffest resistance of the whole war. We were shelling East Jerusalem from the Israeli side and it was pretty tough going.

'I went into a house to ring my wife. All the inhabitants were in the shelter. I went down myself and asked for the proprietor. An old Orthodox Jew came up with me to the ground floor and asked me what I wanted. I asked for his permission to use the telephone.

' "The telephone?" he repeated.

' "I want to ring my wife," I told him.

'He was surprised.

' "Your wife?" he asked.

' "Yes, my wife. In Beersheba."

' "What for?"

' "To tell her that I am all right."

'He grew more and more astonished.

' "There is a battle raging and you want to phone your wife? . . . Go ahead, soldier, by all means. Phone your wife."

'I lifted the receiver, asked for the Beersheba number and got it with less delay than in peace-time. Few people were using the phone that day it seemed. My wife answered, and told me that all was quiet in Beersheba. But hardly had we started talking when three Israeli guns just outside the house opened up and I couldn't hear one single word she was saying. So I went out to the gunners and told them:

' "For goodness' sake. . . . I'm trying to talk to my wife. . . . Could you keep quiet for a bit?'

' "But of course," said the Lieutenant in charge, and firing stopped.

'The old Orthodox Jew watched all this with increasing despair and disbelief. Then he threw up his arms to heaven and exclaimed:

' "This is a Yiddish Army . . . God Almighty, have mercy upon us!" '

Jewish Atrocities

An Arab journalist from East Jerusalem – now enjoying the facilities open to all journalists, including the amenities of the Government Press Office – had some grievance and made a complaint to the head of that office.

'Very well, I'll look into it,' said the Israeli official but the Arab went on and on, harping on his grievance. At last the Israeli official lost his patience.

'Listen,' he said to the Arab, 'you have this minor complaint and you feel very aggrieved. Would *you* have allowed Israeli journalists to become full and equal members of the Jordanian Government Press Office? If you had won the war, what would *you* have done to *us*?'

'Oh,' the Arab replied airily, 'we would have cut your throats, of course. But that's rather different, don't you see? You are civilized and we are not.'

*   *   *

The Arab journalist was right to be sarcastic. I always got impatient when Israelis, accused of atrocities or excesses, retorted: 'But what would the Arabs have done?' It is true that the murderous plans of the Arabs make their complaints (complaints actually made by the would-be killers) a shade less effective and convincing; but when these charges are made by outsiders, who planned no murders, one feels that planned Arab massacres have really nothing to do with the actual Israeli conduct. If the Israelis want to be regarded as civilized people, they have to behave like civilized people, whatever the

89

Arabs may have planned; or, conversely, if they are capable of organized atrocities and murdering innocent people, they have no justification for complaining that people meant to treat them in the way they are ready to treat others.

Do the Israelis, in fact, behave like a civilized nation? Some atrocities were probably committed by individual soldiers on both sides. A war preceded by such emotional excitement is unlikely to have been fought strictly according to Queensberry's rules. The Israeli army, nevertheless, apart from a few individual excesses, respected the rules and behaved on the whole with commendable restraint and fairness. The soldiers were not exactly glad to be called upon to do this job; but they were not incensed and they are not a bloodthirsty lot. I never heard – as I mentioned before – of even one single charge of rape. As I also said before – but it is worth repeating – anyone travelling around the West Bank can sense the easy, relaxed atmosphere. You cannot be misled: there is bitterness and red-hot anger in the Gaza Strip but an almost happy-go-lucky air on the West Bank. I do not mean to say that people are happy; I do not mean that even improved economic conditions for the majority compensate for the national humiliation. No nation enjoys being occupied by its worst enemy. Yet, there is no denying it: occupiers and occupied are getting along without any major friction, much better than anyone dared to expect.

My impression grew into firm conviction as I saw more and more of the West Bank; but then I grew suspicious of myself. Was I not being too credulous? – just a mug who falls for anything? Was I being taken for a ride by Israeli propaganda? But I was not exposed to Israeli propaganda. They never said anything more to me than: 'Go wherever you want to, and see for yourself.' I watched out for signs of atrocities and oppression. I did hear two main stories: the wanton destruction of four Arab villages; and the blowing up of houses belonging to terrorists.

I saw the story of the four Arab villages in a number of reputable newspapers – including the *Sunday Times* of June 16, 1968. According to this story, the Israelis destroyed four villages – Zeita, Beit Nuba, Yalu and Imvas (or Emmaus, of biblical fame) in a callous and brutal manner. Bulldozers had been used – we were told – to cover up all trace of where these villages had stood. The writer of the *Sunday Times* article, Mr Michael Adams, a well-known expert on the Middle East and a journalist of excellent reputation, got a substantial part of his information from local Arabs, purporting to be eye-witnesses. His report ends with these emotional words:

'In days to come, no doubt, young Israelis in search of a picnic site will take the ancient road to Emmaus and spread themselves under these trees and laugh and take their ease. But there will be ghosts among the branches. For here, if anywhere, stood "thy neighbour's landmark".'

This article drew a reply from the Israeli Embassy in London which stated that the villages had suffered heavy damage 'during the June war and its immediate aftermath', when Israeli troops engaged two Egyptian commando units established there; these commandos continued fighting after the cease-fire. Having said that much about the matter under discussion, the writer of the letter continued with the usual irrelevancies: what the Arabs would have done had *they* won the war. He declared that thirty-two synagogues had been demolished or desecrated in the Old City of Eastern Jerusalem. Finally he added that it would have been more worthwhile to comment on Israel's lack of rancour in word and deed, etc, etc.

Such evasion of the proper issues created the strong impression that Israel has something to hide. The reference to hypothetical Arab atrocities read, in this context, as justification for actual Israeli atrocities; the demolition of thirty-two synagogues in Eastern Jerusalem, like the flowers that bloom in the spring, have nothing to do with the case. Except, once again, if Arab atrocities justify Jewish vengeance. Finally, Mr Adams was free to choose what subjects he should write on. He did not want to write about the lack of Israeli rancour; he chose the destruction of four Arab villages – an important enough theme.

I turned to the Israeli military authorities for further enlightenment. They did give me a few meagre facts but beyond that their attitude was: 'No comment'. The military spokesman – and the government spokesman – both confirmed that the four villages had, in fact, been destroyed; they no longer existed and the sites had been bulldozed. That was all and it looked very bad indeed.

In the end I discovered what I accept as the truth. I got my information and my evidence partly from official sources who did not allow me to quote them and partly from other 'well-informed circles' who should know and whose data confirmed the other sources. I did not see the villages, of course, as there is nothing left to see; I could not trace any Arab survivors as they are dispersed. All my information comes from Israeli sources and there are gaps in my knowledge. All I can say is that personally I am satisfied and I believe that I know the truth. And the truth seems to be this.

Three days before the outbreak of the war (June 2, 1967) Egyptian commandos hid themselves in these villages and committed acts of sabotage. After the outbreak of hositilities these acts continued and the four Jordanian villages were attacked by advancing Israeli forces. The attacks were legitimate acts of war. As soon as the Israelis entered the villages the Egyptian commandos donned pyjamas and, having become indistinguishable from the Arab inhabitants of the neighbourhood, fled and disappeared in the crowd. After the war, however, they returned, used the ruins as a hide-out and fired on vehicles and convoys using the main Jerusalem road. As the ruins provided ideal hiding places for the commandos, the Israeli army decided to flatten them; the houses had become uninhabitable in any case. The villages were, in fact, completely destroyed and the ground bulldozed. The inhabitants were sent away and they were not properly rehoused.

This story has been retold in innumerable newspaper articles. The reader may think that the original destruction was a proper act of war; that the final destruction was justified; he may also think that the Arab inhabitants should have been taken care of and treated in a less callous manner. But let us, in any case, remember: *it is always the story of the same four villages.*

Immediately after my return from Israel I read a reference to these villages in an article by the Israeli journalist, Mr Amos Kenan, in the July 12, 1968, number of the *New Statesman and Nation*. He said that he had actually taken part – or had been ordered to take part – in the destruction of these villages: and had been so outraged by these orders that he deserted his unit and wrote a report on this action. Copies of his report were sent to the General Staff, to members of the Government and the Knesset. Very few Russian soldiers wrote similar reports, one assumes, when they were ordered to invade Czechoslovakia: and if one or two did, they were not privileged to tell the story in the *New Statesman*. Mr Kenan's indiscipline was treated differently. He – a private – was ordered to report before the General commanding his division who handed Private Kenan a full, written report and told him that what had happened had been a regrettable error of judgement which would not occur again. Mr Kenan was reluctant to believe the General, suspecting that he was trying to conceal other, similar occurrences. He asked the General how it might be ensured that similar 'errors' would not occur again? The General signed an order on the spot, permitting Mr Kenan free movement in all the occupied territories so that he could investigate and see things with his own eyes. He did so and found that, indeed, no similar acts had been committed anywhere else. Mr Kenan goes on: 'But since then, in all the peace papers in the world, my report about the destruction of villages has been reprinted over and over again, as if it happened only yesterday, as if it is happening all the time. And this is a lie. It is like writing that witches have been burnt at the stake in England – omitting the date. I hereby request all those who believed me when I reported a criminal act, to believe me now too. And those who do not believe me now, I hereby request to disbelieve my former report too, and not to believe me selectively, according to their convenience.'

*　　*　　*

The other matter I referred to is the blowing up of houses. The

Jerusalem Post reported on June 27, 1968, that a young man, Jehad Taleb Muhammed Hamdan, aged twenty-one, had been killed as a terrorist six days before. After the death of the young man an Israeli army demolition squad blew up his parents' house in Kafr Kabalan, a village near Nablus. The parents will get no compensation. They have now moved into the house of Jehad's uncle (whose house was also damaged by the explosion but who will get compensation). The parents declared that their son Jehad had left home four years before, had gone to Kuwait and had sent them no money for about two years.

This looked like a particularly cruel act of biblical revenge: to visit the son's crime on the parents. The Government spokesman, however, explained that houses which belonged to terrorists or which sheltered terrorists were being blown up. This was no secret; in fact it was well-advertised Israeli policy and public knowledge. The habit was adopted from the British who also blew up such houses and meted out collective punishment. The Israelis – the spokesman told me – refrained from collective punishment but did blow up houses because it is vitally important for them to discourage terrorism and to discourage people from hiding terrorists. If terrorists have nowhere to hide, terrorism must become ineffective. The house in question was, in fact, Jehad's property, so it was blown up. The spokesman added: 'We do not like this policy. It is distasteful; but it is also successful. We have to protect ourselves so we persist in it as long as necessary.'

*　　*　　*

One may object to the use of the word 'terrorist'. Nothing is more natural than that the Israelis should call them 'terrorists' and the Arabs 'resistance fighters' or 'freedom fighters'. I shall call them guerillas. The West Bank is undoubtedly enemy-occupied territory for the Arabs and a resistance movement is justified. The young men who take part in guerilla activities are patriots and not criminals. But they take risks and must take the consequences. They commit acts of sabotage and they shoot; so the Israelis shoot back and, whenever they can, they shoot first. Any man who goes to war must know that he might get hurt.

It should also be added that Israel has a better record here than any other occupying power. Not one single guerilla has been executed as a punishment, after capture. There are no firing squads in Israel; no hangmen. A guerilla who is caught is safe. (The Arabs say that the Israelis do not execute guerillas because they never take any prisoners. They have no guerillas to execute. They shoot them all before or after they surrender. This would be an extremely stupid policy because a live guerilla is an important source of information; a dead guerilla is not. In any case, such an allegation is hardly compatible with the fact that there are 1,500 Arab guerillas in Israeli prisons.)

* * *

In an occupied village (in Sinai this time) an Israeli officer was reprimanding one of his junior officers because he seemed to be too harsh or unjust in a certain matter. The junior officer tried to justify his conduct but his senior was not satisfied. At last the younger man exclaimed:

'Very well. I have made a mistake. My father was a green-grocer in Cracow and failed to instruct me how to run a military occupation. I am glad that your father brought you up properly.'

* * *

One more word about guerillas, partisans, terrorists – call them what you like. This guerilla movement – let's face it – is pretty ineffectual. There is a lot of smoke but little fire. Of course, there are certain successes; certain scares; some nasty incidents, some deaths – the worst, to date, was an explosion in West Jerusalem in November 1968 but, on the whole, up to the moment of writing this the movement has caused more trouble to Hussein than to Israel.

I talked to a former Jewish terrorist leader, a man who was active before 1948 and famous for it after 1948. A true expert on such matters and, I am afraid, very contemptuous about the Arab achievements.

'Absolute beginners,' he told me on the terrace of a Tel-Aviv café. 'Needless to say, we cannot relax and we must protect ourselves with all the means at our disposal. They do certain things: bombs are discovered in cinemas and the next bomb may not be discovered before it explodes and may kill hundreds of women and children. And men too. There are some explosions; sometimes a succession of small explosions and now and then they cause damage and hurt or kill people. But what they really do is mostly pranks; silly hit-and-run affairs. Antics of adolescents, boy-scout stuff. As soon as some small result *is* achieved, rival organizations start a public quarrel, claiming credit for the deed. Sometimes none of them has anything to do with it. When Dayan hurt himself doing some excavation work, the Arabs claimed it was their achievement. But it was just an accident really. The Arabs only read about it in the newspapers.'

He ordered another fruit juice. He never touches alcohol.

'And when these *fedayun* are caught, they *talk*. They talk voluntarily, freely and volubly, and give away all their secrets; names and everything. They are not tortured; they torture their captors with their verbosity. They vie with another, who knows the most important secrets. It makes them feel important.'

He lit a cigarette and continued: 'We Jews could do this, too, so much better. If I were in charge of the terrorist movement against Israel, people here would live in terror. It would be impossible to journey in safety in this land; no one would dare visit a concert or a cinema; there would be no happy crowds of tourists, unconcernedly seeing the sights. It would be a very different story. A professional job. I'd spread terror and panic in this land.'

He stopped. I expected him to add: 'And God, wouldn't I enjoy it?'

But he said no such thing.

Postscript: while this book was at the printers, guerilla activities were speeded up. There were attacks on El-Al planes in Athens and Zurich, explosions in Jerusalem, etc. In some cases the Arabs made ludicrous claims such as that they were responsible for Eshkol's death. In spite of the increased activities, the foregoing remains true. A visiting Israeli friend told me in 1969: 'Judging by the headlines of London papers we live in fear, but the headlines in Tel-Aviv papers are much smaller. We shrug our shoulders and take the guerillas in our stride. They don't interfere with our daily life.'

Jerusalem

On Wednesday, June 28, 1967, Mr Teddy Kollek became Mayor of Jerusalem and announced that as from 8 a.m. the following day Jerusalem would be a united city once again; all barriers would come down and all the inhabitants would be allowed to move about freely in the city. A large number of people refused to believe their ears: surely, he meant to say that Jews would be permitted to visit East Jerusalem but not that, at the same time – not quite three weeks after the war – Arabs could come over to the West? Yes, Mr Kollek meant precisely that. A united city is a united city for all its inhabitants. Very well, people asked him, but could the Arabs come over in unlimited numbers? Yes, as many as cared to.

Quite a few people were seriously worried. In some cases, young girls were sent to Tel-Aviv and other places by anxious parents fearing rape. The majority of people however had no misgivings; they welcomed the order, trusted the Arabs and proved to be right. June 29, 1967, remains an exciting and memorable day in the history of Jerusalem – a city which has lived with history and has made history for thousands of years.

Only the inhabitants of Berlin, Nicosia and, of course, Jerusalem, appreciate fully what it means to live in a divided city. Jerusalem was divided for twenty years. This means that people under thirty or so – about half the population – remembered not at all or only in the haziest fashion that there was once a time when Jerusalem was like other, normal cities of the world. Only the middle-aged and the old remembered the bygone days when there was no Mandelbaum Gate, no barbed wire, no fortifications in the middle of the town, no hostile sentries with fixed bayonets across the street; when Jews could go to the Old City and Arabs could roam about at will in the modern parts.

What the Israelis longed to see was the Wailing Wall. Orthodox Jews had not had a good wail since the end of the 1948 war. The tough, new Israelis hated this very expression *Wailing Wall*; they are not a nation of wailers, and renamed the place the *Western Wall*. But Wailing Wall or Western Wall, all Israelis – Orthodox Jews or tough young nationalists – are equally attached to, and sentimental about, that not too beautiful monument. The Wailing Wall is just what you would expect – a wall. But there are walls and walls; this is not a particularly lovely wall. The lower part of it consists of large, grey and often chipped stones, the upper part looks like a more recent construction, made of smaller bricks. It is the only part of the Temple that has been left standing. Indeed, it is less than that: it never was actually part of the Temple itself, it is just a relic of the wall which surrounded the Temple Court. The lower part dates from the Second Temple period (first century, AD); the upper part was added later. The Wailing Wall is as holy to the Jews as Bethlehem to Christians or Mecca to Moslems. The Jordanians filled up the square in front of the Wall with ugly slum dwellings and built a public lavatory alongside it. (Most Jewish holy places were similarly desecrated – I saw some of them used as dunghills. Today the Islamic places of worship are treated with respect by the Israelis.) As soon as the clock struck eight on Thursday morning, on June 29, a tremendous crowd surged across the former barriers and made straight for the Wailing Wall. The excitement, happiness and ecstasy of the people reached heights unknown even during the Six Day War. Those who were present – completely irreligious people, even atheists among them – assured me that they will never be able to recall those days without tears in their eyes.

At the same time, shy and slightly bewildered Arab groups made their first, tentative steps towards the Israeli sectors. At first, they trusted the Israelis no more than some Israelis trusted them: was it really safe to cross over or was it a trap full of hidden dangers? They found it safe and thousands of them came. The first large group stopped to watch the traffic lights. There were traffic lights in East Jerusalem, too, but the Israeli traffic lights were different. The red light was accompanied by a little red man who stood there, waiting to cross; when the lights changed for green, the little red man became a little green man who set off to cross the road. The Arab crowds were fascinated; when the little green man started walking, they roared with laughter. Someone started applauding and the applause was taken up by the rest of the astounded group. Great success. The traffic lights with their red and green manikins became one of the great attractions of the day.

Ever since that morning, Jerusalem has remained united. People walk about freely, without hindrance. No Arab creates a sensation in the Western parts; indeed, he is not even noticed. I saw a lonely Orthodox Jew late at night, tramping across the bazaar area of the Old City for a late-night wail. There were no other Israelis anywhere near, but he obviously felt quite safe. No one was ever attacked or, as far as I could find out, even molested. Arab policemen, armed with revolvers, patrol the area, but everyone knows that these solitary Jewish pilgrims would be just as safe without a police guard. During the day, little Arab boys attach themselves to the tourists and sightseers, delivering their little sales talks in excellent English or Hebrew and they obviously know more about the Via Dolorosa and Christ's last journey than the average Christian priest, living outside Jerusalem. Sometimes little Arab children play with little Jewish children and the sun does not stand still and the heavens do not fall down. Old Polish Jews who stop to watch Arabs sitting in the street, smoking their *narghile*, are often invited to have a go at the pipe. They accept.

Jerusalem is now part of Israel; many people regard this incorporation as a wanton breach of international law but the Israelis are neither impressed nor unduly worried by this attitude. Jerusalem *always* – even in Ottoman times – had a Jewish majority; East Jerusalem never became part of Jordan and Jordan has no proper claim to the city. Israelis fail to see why Christians should be happier to see the holy places in

Moslem than in Jewish hands. Jerusalem is a holy city of three great religions, each of which has held it in turns. The Jews were deprived of Jerusalem for about 2,000 years. It's their turn now, they feel. Besides, long before the word *Zionism* was uttered for the first time, old religious Jews came from all over the world to die in Jerusalem. It is the finest place to die in – it has always been acknowledged. It has a *joie de mourir* quite its own.

Jerusalem is not only one of the most famous but also one of the most curious cities in the world. It has 266,000 inhabitants: 200,000 Jews, 54,000 Moslems and 11,000 Christians. It has more old people than any other city in Israel, yet the birthrate is double that of the virile new city, Tel-Aviv. It has a very large number of people with academic degrees; it also has an unusually large proportion of illiterates. (Many Oriental Jews settle there.) There is a huge community of militant, religious zealots who are determined to convert other Jews to their own way of life; it also has a large, vociferous and equally militant anti-religious element which is almost anti-semitic in its dislike of the zealots. Jerusalem houses more Christian denominations than Rome, including Greek Orthodox, Russian Orthodox (two varieties) and Roumanian Orthodox Churches; Roman Catholics, Greek Catholics, Maronites, Syrian Catholics, Armenian Catholics and Chaldeans; Monophysite Churches, like the Armenian Orthodox, Coptic, Syrian and Ethiopian Orthodox Churches; Anglicans, Lutherans, Baptists, the Church of Scotland, the Church of the Nazarene, the Pentecostal Movement, the Adventist Church, the Church of Christ, the Church of God, the Quakers, the Christian Brethren and the Mennonites. Twenty per cent of the Arabs are also Christians, the rest are Moslem. Jerusalem is a sacred city of Islam, just as it is a sacred city of Christianity and Judaism. The Harem esh Sharif, the El Aksa Mosque and the Dome of the Rock yield in importance only to Mecca and Medina.

Jerusalem is a beautiful city; an Oriental city; but not a tolerant city. But even in its intolerance it is unpredictable: everyone expected a fearful crime wave after unification but no crime wave followed. Intolerant Arabs live peacefully side

by side with intolerant Jews and intolerant Christians. The Arabs are law-abiding and co-operative, doing a roaring business with foreign and Israeli tourists. If they hate this new situation they certainly do not show it. The Jews rather like them and the numerous Oriental Jews are, in many ways, nearer to the Arabs than to European Jews. (In August 1968 several small bombs exploded, the work of one of the guerilla organizations. The situation looked ugly: an angry crowd wanted to invade the Arab quarters to mete out rough justice. The police prevented them; tempers cooled soon and everything returned to normal.)

The nasty, commercial Jewish spirit – as anti-semites like to picture it – survives only among some of the Christian denominations. Many of the Churches in Jerusalem (and Bethlehem) are divided between various Christian sects and competition is as fierce between them as it is in the plastic or the washing powder trades. The division is often between Roman Catholics, Greek Orthodox and Armenians, but other competitors come in too. There is a territorial division – which part belongs to whom – and a division in time: who can say mass when. The result is that some of these sacred and hallowed places resemble the bazaars outside rather than shrines of great holiness. In the Church of the Holy Sepulchre, Christ's actual burial place is shared between the Greek Orthodox and the Coptic Church. In the Coptic half there is a sign:

THIS IS THE ORIGINAL ROCK OF THE TOMB
IF YOU WANT TO GIVE A DONATION PUT IT HERE

On the plate five and ten pound notes are displayed so that people may be induced to give more. Exactly as in the cloakrooms of big hotels.

The West Bank: Two Mayors

In 1929 there was a massacre of Jews in the town of Hebron. The mayor of Hebron then was Sheikh Muhammad Ali Jabari. When the Israeli army entered Hebron thirty-eight years later, the town awaited its arrival in terror. There was not a soul in the streets; all the shops were closed; there was not a single official in the Town Hall or any other public office; there was hardly any sign of life. The Israeli military commander sent loudspeaker vans around the town and summoned the Mayor and the high officials to the Town Hall. Thirty-eight years had passed, but Muhammad Ali Jabari was still mayor. He and his officials assembled in front of the Military Commander. The Mayor said coolly and factually to the Commander: 'You've come for revenge.' He was neither afraid nor disapproving.

'Perhaps,' said the Commander.

All in the room remained silent for a long time. Then the Israeli Commander spoke again.

'I am prepared to make you an offer, Mr Mayor. If you guarantee the safety of my soldiers – all of them, without one single exception – I'll guarantee the safety of all your citizens.'

'I accept that,' nodded the Mayor coldly and without any emotion. He was a member of one of the great Palestine families who have dominated the country for centuries. He had seen the Turks in Palestine; then the British; then the Jordanians. Now the Israelis. Conquerors come and go but Hebron has been there since biblical times and before; Hebron is eternal. And he, as Mayor, almost eternal. The Mayor was used to giving orders and the citizens of Hebron were used to accepting them. The deal was struck. Not one Israeli soldier was attacked;

not one citizen of Hebron suffered because of 1929. (There was an incident in September 1968 – but no one blamed the local Arabs.)

When I went to see the Mayor of Hebron, he was waiting for me on the steps of the Town Hall. He was elegantly attired in traditional Arab garb and the *kefiyah*, the Arab headgear. I knew he must be an old man but he looked ageless. He received me with perfect but icy courtesy, without a smile, without any sign of pleasure or displeasure. He has cunning and suspicious eyes and can be as impersonal as a piece of furniture or a document: the document conveys certain meanings to you but you can never fathom its feelings and deeper emotions. The Mayor looked inscrutable, unafraid, uncommunicative and noncommittal. As soon as we sat down, he pressed – imperceptibly as he thought – a button to set an invisible tape-recorder in motion. Most politicians and public men have learnt the art of saying nothing in many words; the Mayor of Hebron has learnt the greater art of saying nothing in very few words.

As we went on talking, more and more people – all of them Arabs – came into the room. We were introduced, shook hands and they, too, were served coffee and cold drinks by humble servants.

I asked the Mayor if he could say something about the problems confronting him.

'Are you writing a book or just articles?' was his answer.

I told him I was writing a book.

Silence.

I asked him once again, through his interpreter (he insisted on talking Arabic) if he could say something about his problems.

'What problems?' he asked. Had he been able to show any emotion at all, his voice would now have reflected faint surprise. Problems?

I replied that I thought the occupation of his city by a foreign army might have created some problems.

'No problems at all,' said the Mayor impassively. 'Everything is going on smoothly.'

I asked if he had any criticism to make against the occupation authorities.

'No criticism at all.'

'What about the closing of the banks?'

He looked in my direction but not into my eyes: 'The closing of the banks affects the economic situation.'

'Are people better off or worse off under the occupation?'

'Worse off.'

'What are the difficulties, then?'

'Goods are not being let in freely from the East Bank,' he said and I felt almost proud of getting that much out of him.

'What sort of solution do you envisage, Mr Mayor?'

'The Arabs and Israel together will find some solution.'

'But *what* solution can that be?'

He looked in my direction again: 'The United Nations may help.'

'Do you think the formation of an independent Arab Palestine a feasible idea?'

'That's up to the people of Palestine.'

Then he added: 'Such a solution, however, must also have the approval of the Israeli Government.'

'Have you got at least minor complaints? Minor problems?'

'All issues are being dealt with by me and the occupation authorities.'

At this moment two high-ranking Israeli officers came into the room. When they realized that the Mayor was being interviewed, they offered to withdraw, so that the Mayor should be able to speak his mind freely. I begged them to stay because I felt the Mayor – their presence notwithstanding – would go on speaking just as freely as before. He did. He went on in the same vein for another five minutes or so. I thanked him for having received me and left.

The Mayor of Hebron had the reputation of being a man friendly to the occupation authorities. I was told in Amman he was regarded as a collaborator and that he had burnt all his bridges and was in grave, personal danger if the Jordanians returned. This seems nonsense to me. The Mayor of Hebron is a feudal seigneur; he likes no one; he respects no one; he fears no one. He does not 'collaborate' with anyone. He has seen Turks, British and Jordanians come and go; he has now seen Israelis come and is convinced that they will go, too. He does not want to solve the problems of the Arab world; he is not worried by the problems of Egypt and Jordan; he has no sleepless nights because of the future of the Middle East. The world is not his oyster. He cares for Hebron, and Hebron only, which he regards more or less as his personal property. He is a big enough man not to be concerned about the whole wide world and to care for his own city alone.

Perhaps, who knows, deep down in his heart he may even feel a tiny bit of affection for Hebron.

* * *

The Mayor of Nablus, Sheikh Hamdi Chanaan, is a very different person. Of all mayors on the West Bank it was only he and the Mayor of Hebron who hit the headlines of the world press. The Mayor of Hebron has the reputation of compromising with the occupation forces, the Mayor of Nablus of being a staunch and adamant Arab nationalist. My feeling is that though they speak with very different tongues, they act in the same way: they are both looking after the interests of their own people. Perhaps the Mayor of Nablus has in addition some personal ambition, and thinks of his future while the Mayor of Hebron feels contempt for a motive like ambition and knows that his future is behind him.

The Mayor of Nablus is a self-made man, not a member of one of the great established families. So he has to prove himself, all the time. He, too, received me in his office at the Town Hall. He wore European clothes and spoke in English, bringing in his interpreter only when he could not find the right word.

'We never expected the occupation to last so long,' these were his first, complaining words. I was surprised. I was tempted to ask: 'Had you known it would last so long, you would not have agreed to be occupied?'

But I said nothing of the kind and he went on. He called the occupation 'colonization'. He said it brought financial hardship to the people, higher taxes, unemployment, etc. Occupation also disrupted family life, as many people had fled to the East Bank. There was another reason, the Mayor explained, for further hardships: many Palestine Arabs had gone to Kuwait, Libya and other prosperous places, had good jobs there and used to send large sums of money back to support their parents and aged relatives.

'They refuse to send any more money,' said the Mayor. 'They are not sure that the money will reach their families.'

'But it would. You know it would.'

'I know but they don't. And that's the point.'

'True. But you could tell them.'

'No use. In any case they do not want to support the Israeli economy.'

'That seems to be fair enough, Mr Mayor,' said I. 'But don't they want to support their parents?'

'Not if it means supporting the Israeli economy, too.'

'But isn't it true, Mr Mayor, that while the Israeli economy will not starve because of their lack of support, their parents might?'

'It is the duty of the occupation forces to look after the people here.' He added that people were hard up, many were living on their savings and those savings would not last long. Earnings were still very low, taxes high.

I asked the Mayor what solution did he see?

Everyone wanted peace, he replied. But a military occupation did not serve peace. So Israel should withdraw, without delay. *After that*, the Arab states would reach a solution. Even if they did not, why should the ordinary people suffer and remain under foreign occupation? Israeli occupation was a grave threat to peace.

'Are you in favour of peace negotiations between Arabs and Israel?' I asked him.

'Yes, but only if the Arab states want to negotiate.'

'Are you in favour of negotiating a separate peace? Forming an independent, Arab Palestine?'

'No, not that. We are part of Jordan. A tiny, independent Palestine would in any case not be viable. We want to be reunited with Jordan.'

He emphasized that all Arab countries must be parties to a solution. His main theme was that the occupation itself was the beginning and the end: it was the root of all evil, so it must cease. Israel must give in on this point. A withdrawal would help to achieve a solution. I asked him about El Fatah; he said it consisted mostly of Palestinian Arabs and was a legitimate resistance movement.

'Would you agree, Mr Mayor,' I asked him, 'that Israeli occupation is the mildest ever occupation in history?'

'All occupation is evil.'

'I am sure of that. Nevertheless, do you agree that Israeli occupation is the mildest ever known in history?'

'The mildest?' he repeated my word.

'You speak very freely and bravely, Mr Mayor. But isn't the fact that you can speak like this to a foreign journalist proof in itself that the authorities are lenient and tolerant? You are allowed to call El Fatah a legitimate resistance movement. Not all occupation authorities would be quite as liberal as that. Or don't you agree?'

He shook his head.

'I don't. The occupation, it is quite true, has certain lighter aspects. Not all occupations are equally oppressive in all fields. There is a certain amount of freedom of speech here and that is one of the lighter aspects of this particular oppression. But there are harsher aspects, too. Besides, I can say whatever I like but not everybody can. People had to flee or have been punished because of their views. I would not remain Mayor of Nablus if I was not allowed to speak my mind. I would not become anybody's puppet.'

The two Israeli officers – who had come and heard the second part of this interview – nodded in approval. Everybody liked the Mayor of Nablus, I felt. The Jordanians liked him: a true and fearless patriot, obviously nobody's puppet; and the Israelis liked him even more: with his anti-Israeli tirades he was the best of advertisements for Israeli tolerance. An honest and brave man, let there be no doubt about that, with his fearless, outspoken criticism, he was doing more good to Israel than to the Arab cause.

Golan Heights

We arrived at the first Syrian village and memories of the London blitz returned most vividly. I saw demolished walls, houses which had collapsed like cardboard and rooms with one wall missing, like stage sets; houses with their roofs shaved off; signs of shelling and fires and desolation everywhere. The place we stopped at first had been a Syrian officers' mess; now it was an Israeli roadside café.

I wandered around and walked deep into the woods, passing on the way an Israeli sentry who looked at me impassively and said nothing. When I returned, a stranger informed me that he was pleased – or, at any rate, surprised – to see me come back in one piece. The whole area had been infested with mines; the mines had not been cleared from the wood. I asked this man why the soldiers failed to warn me. 'Oh,' he said, 'our soldiers do not like to interfere with foreign journalists. It makes a bad impression.'

Golan is a very different place from the West Bank. The West Bank bustles with life, Golan is dead. The West Bank – while not the happiest place on earth – is neither bitter nor tense: it is relaxed; Golan is neither happy, nor unhappy; it is neither gay nor lugubrious. Golan has no atmosphere. Golan is dead. The entire Arab population departed with the retiring Syrian troops, leaving only six thousand Druse behind. The Druse hate the Syrians and, hearing that their brethren were well treated in Israel, they refused to go. (Now, as a result, the Druse remaining in Syria, are treated worse still.)

Driving through villages you see the shops closed, houses deserted, shutters pulled down, improvised iron bars fixed on the doors to protect property during the temporary absence of the owners. You see Syrian guns and armoured cars and ordinary private motor vehicles in the ditches, rusting away; telegraph poles lying across the unploughed fields; here and there a solitary Druse riding a melancholy donkey or a lonely goat in front of a Druse house.

We passed one or two ghost villages. They had an eerie atmosphere: completely abandoned, decaying, rusting, crumbling and tumbling down in weird silence, broken by mysterious creaks, the last sighs of dying matter. Strange thoughts must pass through all travellers' heads: some must expect ghosts to appear at any moment, with green faces, dressed in long, white Arab garments; others may hear owls hooting; I – being a man of less tragic disposition – expected rather something like Act One of *Ruddigore* with departed souls cracking jokes and singing and dancing.

One passes Syrian army camps, now occupied by the Israeli army. Kuneitra, the largest, indeed the only, town of the territory, is also derelict. The shopping district is closed to the public (that means tourists), the Israeli army protects the property of the rightful owners against theft but not against decay. The occupation forces have also launched some *kibbutzim*. It is not – we are told – that the Israelis are trying to repopulate these regions. Oh no. But the boys and girls in the army are bored; why should they not be allowed to pass their time usefully, growing things, leading creative lives, instead of just sitting around gaping vacantly and drinking – particularly as Jewish soldiers do not drink. These new *kibbutzim* at Golan, we were told, are very different from the ordinary, Israeli *kibbutzim*, where people mean to stay for ever. This is no doubt so. I personally failed to detect any differences. But I am no expert on *kibbutzim*.

Then we stopped to examine the fortifications. They seemed impregnable. The Heights dominate the Jordan valley: any attacker must climb up, any defender could shoot downwards. An attacker met first a line of barbed wire, then minefields and then the more formidable obstacles: fortified buildings with gun- and machine-gun positions. These places were manned day and night. Thick concrete roofs protected the buildings against aerial attack and they had special protection against napalm bombs too. Behind such a row of fortifications there was another line of barbed wire, another line of minefields and another row of fortified buildings – and so on, in great depth. The guns formed a complicated pattern and could (and did) make life hell in the settlements of Galilee. The system seems unassailable. In earlier estimations of the Israeli General Staff, its conquest would have cost so many lives, that it was out of the question even to consider a frontal attack. In the end, when the frontal attack came, the defence collapsed in two days, the Syrian army fled in panic and the Golan Heights were conquered at the cost of two hundred lives.

Surely, this is one of the most incredible stories of that incredible war. So people invented an explanation – I heard it repeatedly, always told with a great air of confidence. Syria, the story runs, had a secret pact with Israel. Syria agreed to withdraw to a certain line and Israel, for her part, promised not to advance beyond this line and, particularly, not to take Damascus. This contention is proved – I was told – also by indirect evidence: (1) The Syrians – as everyone who has studied this matter knows – actually announced the fall of Kuneitra long before Kuneitra fell, proof that they knew Kuneitra would fall; and (2) nowadays the Syrians do not complain about refugees and are involved in no quarrels with Israel and there are no frontier incidents between Syria and Israel. This story, I hasten to add, is unmitigated nonsense. There are people for whom politics and war are a series of conspiracies and secret pacts taken from the cheaper type of spy novel. Real life occasionally follows these novels: Mao keeps talking of a secret conspiracy between the United States and the Soviet Union to carve up and dominate the world; according to the Russians, there was a secret conspiracy between Dubček – a more faithful Communist than Brezhnev – and the Americans; according to *Pravda*, there were American paratroopers in Prague before the Russians arrived; according to Nasser, English and American planes took part in conspiratorial air-raids against Egypt during the Six Day War, and I heard one Sudanese patriot deliver a lecture on a Zionist-Arab conspiracy against his country. It is a pleasant, if somewhat puerile, game to try to prove that those who seem to be deadly enemies are in fact secretly in cahoots. But if we leave the world of spy fiction we must ask: why should Syria – possessing impregnable fortifications – make secret pacts with her deadly enemy, instead of relying on those fortifications? Syria was and still is the most implacable of all the Arab states; she was the ostensible cause of the whole war (the Russians reported that Israel was about to attack Syria). Why should the Syrians now give away – *voluntarily* – large chunks of their country which they always deemed unconquerable? They could simply have avoided war, as they knew as well as the Russians that no one was thinking of attacking them – not even a retaliatory raid was in preparation. The truth is that the Israelis could not have conquered the Golan Heights a month before the June war; they could not have conquered it a month after it. But after four days of fighting their reputation for invincibility was such that as the Israelis approached the Syrians ran away.

It is quite true, nevertheless, that the fall of Kuneitra *was* announced long before it actually happened. I heard the not improbable explanation that it was announced by the Israelis, using the Damascus wavelengths and pretending to be the Syrian Radio. Other garrisons believed themselves outflanked by the fall of Kuneitra, the central fortress, so they fled. It is also true that nowadays there are no – or very, very few – incidents between Israelis and Syrians. But the Syrians are just as hostile as before; they are arming El Fatah and send the guerillas to Jordan because the Syrian-Israeli frontiers are utterly unsuited for infiltration. Then again, it is understandable that the Syrians should not want to complain about refugees and incidents: they are too deeply hurt and even more sensitive about their crushing defeat than the others.

There was no conspiracy; there is, today, the usual, hopeless situation. The Syrians refuse to negotiate without withdrawal; the Israelis refuse to withdraw without prior negotiations. The Israelis are accused of being cynical: it is said that Syrian (and all Arab) intransigence suits them only too well. Conceivably. But they are not responsible for Arab intransigence. It is up to the Arabs to stop being intransigent and call the Israelis' bluff – if bluff it is. . . .

The Syrians refuse to budge because they insist on their sacred rights. But 'sacred' is a dangerous word in politics – it is dangerous enough in religion, too. In politics it simply means unreasonable. He who has sacred rights is entitled to expect a miracle. Miracles, of course, often occur, but cases are known when they don't.

Gaza

Travelling south from Tel-Aviv, you pass through the fast-growing town of Ashdod and pleasant little Ashkelon, full of well-dressed and immaculately clean Oriental Jews; you see the road sign pointing towards the *kibbutz* Yad Mordechai and then you cross the former frontier to the Gaza strip.

You have arrived in a new world. You have travelled not only a few miles south-west but also quite a few hundred years back in time. The industrialized, computer-ridden twentieth century is behind you; or, if you happen to look in the other direction, hundreds of years ahead of you. There are a few well-built houses but they are scattered amid ramshackle huts and collapsing shacks. You see donkeys and camels and women carrying huge pitchers on their heads. For a moment you wonder what the introduction of running water will do to the inimitable grace of these Arab women? It is the habit of carrying pitchers on their heads which makes their gait so graceful and elegant. But you dismiss this frivolous thought and are ashamed of it. Besides, there is no danger. Many a year will pass and these women – and their daughters and grand-daughters – will still be carrying pitchers on their heads. They will remain poor, half-starved, miserable and very, very graceful.

You need spend no more than a few minutes in Gaza to feel the air of utter hopelessness, misery and hatred. This place is exactly what you expected *all* the Israeli-occupied territories to be before you set out on your journey. But in Jerusalem and on the West Bank you found a surprisingly relaxed and easy-going atmosphere; in Golan you found no population under

occupation. But here the very air is electric: there is hatred in people's eyes, bitterness in their hearts, a desire for revenge in every word they utter and despair and despondency as regards their future.

The population of the former Gaza Strip consists of the original pre-1948 population of Palestinian Arabs, plus those who arrived, or whose parents arrived, as refugees after the first Jewish-Arab War. There were about 400,000 people here after the Six Day War, but 50,000 have moved over to Jordan. The Israelis encourage such moves and even give a few pounds to those who are about to depart, but the Jordanians – understandably – are not enthusiastic about absorbing still more refugees. Some of the Gaza Strip refugees can see their own former homes across the border, and the new Israeli proprietor ploughing their land. The overwhelming majority of the people live on meagre UNWRA rations and have little hope that their future will differ from the past two decades. Indeed, under Israeli rule their position has become much worse: chances of employment have decreased; much less money is received from relatives in Arab countries; and UNWRA itself is in a pretty bad financial state. On top of all that, the export of citrus fruit has ceased and prices have fallen disastrously. Gaza used to sell its oranges and lemons to East Germany and other members of the Eastern bloc. Today no trade is possible with these countries and if they can sell anything at all to Western countries, they get very low prices because their fruit is of poor quality compared with the best Israeli citrus fruit. The commerce of the Gaza Strip is dying. Gaza used to be almost a free port and people from Cairo and Ismailia and Port Said used to come here to do their shopping. Nobody comes any more. There is nothing to buy.

'Our future?' an intelligent and comparatively moderate Palestinian Arab said to me, one of the lucky ones who had a reasonably good job – 'We ask ourselves this question every day, every hour. We just don't know. We are in a hopeless mess.'

'You still hope to get back your property in Israel?'

'Oh no. Not in *Israel*. They took our land, they took our

houses. They robbed us. They must give our property back. That's the only solution.'

'But you know perfectly well that they won't give your property back. Some other solution must be found. Some compromise.'

'There can be no compromise. They stole our fatherland. They must give it back.'

I asked him if he had been happier under Egyptian rule. It is well known that the people in the Gaza Strip were not accepted as Egyptian citizens and were treated rather harshly in many ways. They needed travel permits to go to Egypt. Yet, his answer was unhesitating.

'It was far better. There was a chance of higher education – our sons could go to Cairo University. All that's gone now. We did need a permit to travel but it was very easy to get.' (This was exaggeration. Only very few people could go to Cairo University and travel permits were not all that easy to obtain.) 'I did not feel oppressed as I feel today. I was a free man. Today I cannot forget for a moment that I live under military occupation. The Egyptians were no angels. They did not do as much for us they ought to have done. But they were our own people. Our kith and kin. I felt at home.'

I talked to many people, my notebooks are full of conversations I jotted down. Most of them were even more bitter; not a single person was more tolerant. I did not hear one word of hope; not one single remark to suggest that some compromise solution might be possible. A former well-to-do peasant – now a shoe repairer who had very few shoes to repair – told me:

'I would not go back to Israel as long as the Jews are there. I'd rather die.'

'Even if you got all your property back?'

'Yes. I'd rather die than live under Israeli rule.'

'Would you accept resettlement in an Arab country?'

'I would not. Why should I? I want my own land back and nothing else.'

'You would not accept it even if Arab governments asked you to accept it?'

'No. I want my own land back.'

'You live under Israeli rule now.'

'They may go one day. In any case: *they* have come here. *I* certainly would not go to live in Israel.'

'Do you see any solution?' I asked.

'We trust in God. He will give us back our land.'

'When?'

'One day. God is never in a hurry.'

I talked to a number of other men. All expressed the same attitude. I also met a schoolboy of sixteen, born there as a refugee, of refugee parents.

'It was much better before the war. Now you see your enemy every day. And you can't do anything about it. This is a horrible life. It's humiliating. The other day Jewish soldiers surrounded our school and broke in by force.'

'Why?'

'No reason at all.'

'There must have been some reason.'

'Some boys threw stones at them from the upper floor. But the real reason was that some students had demonstrated in the town a week before. An armoured jeep drove into the courtyard and they tried to force the door. The boys were terrified. The soldiers could not get in, so they sent for reinforcements. In the end they forced their way in and beat up students and masters. Some were badly hurt. One student, I think, died.'

'You *think?*' I asked. 'Surely you would know if a boy from your own form – or at least your own school – died.'

'I think he died.'

I persisted: 'The funeral of a schoolboy killed by Israeli soldiers would be a major event, reported in the world press. And the Arab press would certainly make a lot of it. It all happened in this town. Was there a funeral? Did you go to a funeral?'

He did not reply.

'You must know that. Did you go to a boy's funeral? Did you hear of a funeral? Do you know the name of the boy who is supposed to have died?'

'I don't know his name but I think a boy died.'

'What are your plans for the future?'

'I want to be a soldier. I want to fight the Jews.'

An Israeli officer told me: 'This is an awful place. Security comes first; next after security comes our endeavour to make friends with the population. We have been successful with security; but we have completely failed in our attempt to be friendly. Tension is kept up artificially. Throwing stones is a favourite pastime. Incidents are provoked, then a curfew is imposed. We arrest people. This creates more bitterness, new incidents, another curfew, new arrests. And so on. It is all engineered from outside – although people here are bitter enough without any outside encouragement.'

'So all the faults are on the Arab side?'

'Oh no. We make mistakes. Some time ago people were throwing stones, as usual, at passing Israeli cars but this time they used young Arab girls to do it. One Israeli civilian – I think a chap from Ashdod – got frightened, drew his revolver, fired and the bloody fool wounded five Arab girls. This was quite mad although I must admit that in this atmosphere nerves snap easily.'

I watched the distribution of the miserable UNWRA rations: 1,500 calories per day (1,600 in winter) distributed once a month. Every grain of rice, every broad bean, every drop of soya-bean oil is watched anxiously.

Off the main streets, dirty and hungry people squat in front of their miserable, overcrowded huts; old Arabs smoke their pipes in front of places euphemistically called cafés; there are a few goats chained to fences; some chickens flap about in the road when a car passes, beating up clouds of dust; small children go to 'water points' with jugs larger than themselves. People ignore you or stare at you – whether they stare with curiosity or with hatred depends on what they think you are.

The Gaza Strip is a cauldron of hatred. It is even worse than it seems. It was occupied by Israelis after the Suez War of 1956 but was soon afterwards returned to Egypt. Then, forty men were hanged as collaborators. People today have no love for Israel but they show even less love than they feel. Who knows when Israel will evacuate Gaza once again? Few people like to be hanged.

For twenty years, people were fed day by day on hate propaganda. Their frustration and bitterness was real enough but it was exploited and its flames were fanned by an efficient propaganda machine. For twenty years there were bitter arguments between the two sides and their friends in the world press and at the UN. We heard that the Jews had not done enough for these refugees, which is true: that but for Zionism these people would not be refugees at all, which is also true. We heard that the Arabs could have resettled them many times but prefer to keep them as a festering sore, as evidence of Jewish cruelty: that these people are pawns in a political game. All this is true. The Israeli Declaration of Independence asked these people to stay put, 'to keep their place and play their part in the development of the state, with full and equal citizenship. . . .' But the Arab Higher Committee urged them to go away for a short time, to make the task of the Arab armies easier. Many of those who refused to go in spite of all this were forced onto lorries and driven away. An Arab refugee, quoted by *Ad-di-Faa*, a Jordan daily (September 6, 1954), put it succinctly: 'The Arab governments told us: "Get out so that we can get in." So we got out but they did not get in.' King Hussein himself declared on January 17, 1960: 'Since 1948 Arab leaders have approached the Palestine problem in an irresponsible manner. They have not looked into the future. They have no plan or approach. They have used the Palestine people for selfish political purposes. This is ridiculous and I could say even criminal.' He could say; but he does not say it any more.

It is also true that the Arab press and radio pointed out many times what sort of solution they foresaw. To quote one of many utterances (Voice of the Arabs, June 26, 1961): 'The refugees will not return under the protection of the Israel gang but will become a liberated Arab state in which not a single Zionist will have a foothold and which will fly only the flag of the Arabs.' The Israelis, when this problem is discussed, often ask: 'And what about the Jewish refugees? Once well-to-do people who were expelled by various Arab states, penniless?' All cogent arguments. Both sides put their case most effectively.

In the meantime, hundreds of thousands are born, live and die in that vast concentration camp, where there is plenty of militant talk and ferocious self-delusion but no real hope.

Should you remark quietly that these Arabs are *people*, the argument is pushed aside with a supercilious smile as primitive, naïve, sentimental and utterly non-political. 'We've heard that before.' There is no obvious solution to this question. And if in the depths of the night, lying on the floor of his miserable shack, a refugee feels that some sort of settlement might be attempted after all these years, he will be anxious to suppress all such thoughts as fast as they emerge. It's bad enough to be a refugee; one does not want to be a traitor as well.

So they go on being brave and patriotic, believing the impossible, expecting the unattainable. They should not be blamed for nursing hate and feeling murderous: in such circumstances few of us would be capable of sweet reasonableness. Their outlook is to remain refugees; their children will finish school and then settle down to do nothing, just to being refugees too. They put their faith in Nasser. If Nasser fails, in the United Nations. If the United Nations fail, in God. But as my Arab friend in Gaza remarked: 'God is never in a hurry.'

3 PEOPLE

Americans

Americans in Israel occasionally behave as if they owned the place. The explanation for this may be that they do.

Nowadays, it must be admitted, it is on the whole a very good type of American who comes to Israel. The American tourists are thoughtful and interested people, mostly Jews but a fair number of Christians also, now that the places dear to Christian pilgrims are also in Israel. The typical American businessman – the Vice-President type – is still in evidence but he is not the average tourist. The typical American Vice-President thinks he owns the world; the average American tourist is much more modest: he only thinks he owns Israel.

After the Six Day War a new type of American tourist appeared on the scene. An Israeli friend of mine – a land-surveyor in civil life and a commander of armoured units during the war – summed him up in these words.

'Our American friends insisted on telling us what they had done for us during the Six Day War. "D'you know" – this was the sort of thing they said – "d'you know that when I'd go home those days when the war was on I'd tell my wife: never mind supper, Nancy, I want to watch TV. Just imagine that – no supper, I'd just sit there watching television. All I'd have would be a few sandwiches, a couple of sausages, a cheese-burger or two with a couple of beers and some ice-cream – otherwise I just sat there glued to the set watching, without giving food a thought." I would nod, and thank him for his encouraging interest, and start telling him how my unit had been one of the first to break through into East Jerusalem, but he'd start off again: "That's nothing, you ought to have seen people in New York. Boy, they went crazy – just crazy." '

Americans like most things in Israel ('Oh, everything is just wonderful!') except that they would prefer to see Israel more religious. Not that many of them are so religious at home. But somehow they'd like to see Israel, a Jewish state, more religious for *their* money.

The normal American tourist sees America everywhere. He keeps discovering amazing similarities. They look at Mount Zion and exclaim: 'Now isn't it exactly like Zenith Hill in Alabama?' No one ever says it isn't. Or even that it is quite like it, but not *exactly*. In Safed they say: 'Isn't it exactly like Flowers Spring, Nebraska?' Masada, it seems, is exactly like Fort Worth, Texas, and it is difficult to tell the Negev from Arizona. The more percipient traveller, however, does occasionally discern certain nuances of difference. One American lady remarked to her husband that some lake or other in Connecticut was 'exactly like the Dead Sea, except more dead'. Another noticed – at first glance – that Bethlehem (Judah) was very unlike Bethlehem (Pennsylvania).

I was sitting in the lobby of the King David Hotel in Jerusalem and next to me there was an American couple, ready to depart, waiting for a taxi. The husband said:

'You know, Gladys, this is really too bad. We've promised Jean to go and see Tiberias and now here we are, on our way back home, not having seen it.'

'Why is it too bad?' she asked.

'Well, we did promise.'

'I know we did. But we did see it.'

'You don't say.'

'F'course we did.'

'Tiberias?'

'Sure.'

The man shook his head: 'Never. You're pulling my leg.'

'Well, Jack,' said the lady, 'do you remember the place where we had that tough steak? You said you nearly broke your teeth on it.'

'Sure I remember.'

'Well, that was Tiberias.'

Zionists and JSJs

Nasser, his Arab and his Western friends, assure the world that they are not anti-Jewish, only anti-Zionist. Their feelings are shared by many Jews in Israel: they are certainly not anti-semitic either, but many of them are as anti-Zionist as Nasser himself.

Zionism is *passé*, they say: a creed with a useful purpose in the past similar to that played by the fervour of the Italians and Germans for the unification of their countries during the nineteenth century. Zionism had a noble aim, but it has been achieved, the problem has been settled, and the concept has become out-of-date. It is more than two decades since the State of Israel was established, so the bottle of Zionism has either to be filled with new wine or else thrown away.

When I was in Israel a Zionist Congress was in session. Some Israelis remained aloof; a few definitely hostile; most utterly bored. And even a number of the delegates were embarrassed and rather puzzled as to what the meaning of Zionism might be at the end of the sixties.

Well, what should the aims of Zionism be today? Should Israel go on relying on the Jews in the diaspora? Should Israel try to persuade all Jews to pack up, leave their countries and come to Israel? Must Jews living in Britain, America and anywhere else outside Israel, decide between Israel and their homeland and give up either one or the other? Is there a deep question of *identification*, or is this only one of the fashionable in-words? And what about that notorious *double loyalty*?

The first useful step is to recognize that Zionism has utterly different meanings for Jews in Israel, for Jews outside Israel and for non-Jews.

Let's take non-Jews first. When Nasser states that he is not anti-Jewish, only anti-Zionist, he speaks the truth, and nothing but the truth – even if not the whole truth. He is concerned with the state of Israel as a political force in the Middle East and is interested in Jews in New York, London and Amsterdam only in so far as they support Israel. He does not speak the whole truth because he is aware of the full implication of his position. Many of his non-Arab supporters take the same perfectly logical view, and their anti-Israeli attitude is, of course, as respectable as anybody else's pro-Israeli one. But others use these views as a cloak for their anti-semitism, a state of mind they are loathe to admit even to themselves. Anti-Zionism, in many cases, simply *adds a new dimension to anti-semitism*. It makes anti-semitism respectable again, less than three decades after Auschwitz. Thanks to Nasser (and thanks to Israel) one can again be an anti-semite, without being labelled one.

Viewed from Israel, Zionism has changed its meaning many times throughout its existence. The most conspicuous change is this: until recently Israel needed the Jews living in other lands; today, the Jews in other lands need Israel.

Since the Balfour declaration, Zionism has also meant many other things for many people. First it was for many nothing more than what the old joke said it was: one Jew using the money of another Jew to send a third Jew to Palestine. For a long time it had a defensive and apologetic element: rich Jews wanted to get rid of poor Jews, to send them away, in order to make the remaining Jewry more respectable. Zionism was simply a way of fighting anti-semitism at home. With the rebirth of Jewish nationalism (which coincided with the rebirth of Arab nationalism) Zionism put on a new face; the advent of Hitler gave it new meaning; and the establishment of Israel completely changed the picture once again. As Israel's prestige grew, more and more people discovered their Jewishness. People who used to be ashamed of being Jewish, suddenly became proud of it. And the same thing happened again after each war. Today it is not the Jews in the diaspora who lend prestige to Israel but vice versa. The Six Day War created a new wave of converts and, indeed, it created the species of JSJ: Jews Since June.

The main trends in Israel, concerning Zionism, are these:

(1) *Appeasement*: Zionism is dead but let's pretend that it is still alive. We still need the money of the Americans and others and they send it because they are good Zionists. Israel, of course, should stand on her own feet but it would not be too easy to do without all that foreign aid.

We must not insist on *all* Jews outside Israel coming here. They won't. But we need immigrants desperately. We need people. And Western Jews will not come; they are quite happy where they are. The Soviet Union is the only country with a huge reservoir of Jews, more than three million of them, but for political reasons that reservoir cannot be tapped. The Soviet Union is not going to ruin her relationship with the Arabs by letting an 'expansionist' Israel have more soldiers. Nor does Russia wish to offer the world the spectacle of all her Jewish citizens packing up and leaving as soon as they can, when they are supposed to be contented citizens of the Communist Paradise. That would be a little embarrassing. One day we may have fixed and recognized frontiers, so the influx of people will not mean expansionism. Behind these frontiers we may do what we want and then, perhaps, Russia might change her policy; or her leadership. It is unlikely that all Russian Jews will be let out. Perhaps not all wish to come. But many may.

(While talking of Russia, we may note that this changed notion of Zionism has produced yet another phenomenon in one of Russia's satellites. The Polish Government is a completely discredited gang of failures and the Polish people have to put up with a lot of shortages. Even Jews are in short supply in Poland. But anti-semitism is a useful diversion, as many bankrupt governments know only too well, so in Poland we are treated to the edifying spectacle of anti-semitism without Jews. Although I have to add that during the last few months the Polish Government has seemed to come to its senses.)

E

(2) To the appeasers the *Canaanites* and their allies reply: this is pure nonsense. We have nothing to do with the diaspora. Let's forget about them – forget the Jews of Europe and America and make peace with our neighbours. We have much less in common with those faraway Jews and with their ghetto traditions than with the Arabs around us. Israel belongs to the Middle East, so let us become a true Middle Eastern country. If we need immigrants, there are plenty of them available in Arab lands and – after having made peace with them – let's admit them. To speak of a purely Jewish state is racialism, and Jewish racialism is no better than any other.

To this their opponents reply: this may be a pleasing dream but it certainly is not practical policy. Why accuse Israel of racialism when every state in the world claims some sort of ideological content and refuses to be regarded simply as a shelter for anyone who cares to go and live there? Holland is not accused of racialism for being Dutch nor Norway for being Norwegian. No country permits absolutely free immigration, so why should Israel? It's easy to say 'make peace with the Arabs', but to achieve this is quite a task. At the moment, Arabs do indeed wish to settle in Israel but with guns in their hands, and they want first to take over, then to liquidate the state. In the best case, this *Canaanite* idea is the reincarnation of the old-fashioned idea of assimilation. The old, assimilant Jew tried to become (or posed as) an Englishman, a Pole or a German, and tried to forget (or deny) his Jewishness. What individuals have failed to achieve, the *Canaanites* try to achieve *as a nation*. Let us forget – they say – that we are Jews and let's become Middle Easterners, whatever that may mean. Zionism may be dying; but all of us trying to become pseudo-Arabs, or near-Arabs, is going a shade too far.

(3) The followers of the *British school* have different ideas again. They agree that it is hopeless to expect all the Jews in the world to come to Israel. This, they say, is not only impossible but also undesirable. Israel gains tremendous strength by having Jews scattered all over the world and the true aim of Israel is to become the centre of world Jewry. I call this school of thought the 'British' school, because its advocates visualize –

mutatis mutandis – a Jewish Commonwealth of Nations. Israel has at least as much in common with the Jews of America or Italy as Britain has with the inhabitants of Ghana, Singapore and Trinidad-Tobago.

(4) We should also have a look at the *official aims of Zionism* as stated by the Zionist Congress of 1968. These aims are: the unity of Jewish people and the centrality of Israel in its life; the ingathering of the Jewish people from all lands; the strengthening of the State of Israel; the preservation of the identity of the Jewish people through fostering of Jewish and Hebrew education and of Jewish rights everywhere.

As we see, this statement contains some innocent and some debatable generalities but the crux of the matter is the ingathering of the Jewish people from all lands. It is the definite article, the *the*, which makes this problematical. Ingathering Jewish people from all lands – perhaps; ingathering *the* Jewish people from all lands? – well, they just will not ingather.

* * *

Let us turn to the other side of the picture – Zionism as viewed from the outside. This view contains two main problems.

(1) The first is the problem of *identity*. My advice is: forget about it. This is an artificial problem. A man is not an English Jew, an American Jew, a Turkish Jew, a Chinese Jew; a man is a man. His Jewishness may mean a lot of problems and he may have to face them: but they are not problems of identity. He may be persecuted; humiliated; snubbed. But he is what he is and that is the end of it.

(2) The much-debated problem of *double loyalties* is more complicated. The Americans accept people coming from all lands – they have made America the great country it is. They speak of Irish Americans; but it need never occur to them that an Irish American may be a poor American patriot pestered by the grave problems of double loyalties. (The same goes for Canada and Australia.)

And Europe, too, is full of people who are citizens of one country but have come from another. We never hear anything about the double loyalties of naturalized Britons, Germans, Swedes and Afghans. Why then about Jews? I am sure the problem was invented by people who – consciously or subconsciously – were convinced that Jews were incapable of any loyalty at all. In a way this question of double loyalty brands all Jews: it suggests that an English Jew is different from other Englishmen because Israel exists (and for 'English' read any other nationality). So this man has to choose. Between what? Between going to Israel or staying in Britain? But he has chosen. He has stayed in Britain. Or he has to abandon something. What? His Jewishness? But that is his religion, or race, his background: how can he abandon it any more easily than he can abandon his left arm or tone of voice?

(Had he gone to Israel this double loyalty would still have survived. He would most probably have remained a true and sincere friend of Britain. But that would have been regarded as a laudable attachment, not derogatory 'double loyalty'.)

If there is no conflict between two countries, this double loyalty does not matter. Any more or less decent man has not only double loyalties but treble, quintuple and centuple loyalties. One supports many causes, many countries, many fights. I personally am – at the moment – for Britain, the United States, France, Czechoslovakia, Israel, Biafra and – non-politically – Hungary; and I am against the Rhodesian and South African regimes. This leaves me with seven loyalties.

What if there is a conflict? The 'my country right or wrong' kind of patriotism is today not only out of date but is regarded as something despicable. We thought highly of Germans, like Thomas Mann, who turned against their own country during the Nazi regime. We do not condemn Americans who oppose the Vietnam war; we welcome Greeks, Russians (Stalin's own daughter among them) or Portuguese who flee from tyranny and turn against the ruling regimes of their country. Should Britain be involved in a war with Israel, one's loyalties will not be determined by such factors as whether one is an Englishman, a Jew or both but by the nature of the conflict. If Britain – this is, of course, unimaginable – got involved in a Nazi-type of war with Israel, fighting for oppression and genocide, then many Englishmen would turn against Britain and support Israel; if Israel fought a national war of expansion – instead of one in self-defence – and set out to exterminate Arabs, then many Jews would side and fight against Israel. Thus loyalties would become single again.

Leaving such fancies aside, and until such wars break out, our double and sextuple loyalties should be welcome and not condemned.

Our Arabs

A few days before the outbreak of the Six Day War, when huge Arab armies were massing on the borders of Israel and the situation looked dark, quite a few people threw anxious glances towards Nazareth, the main centre of Israeli Arabs. The Arabs had always been a bit of an enigma. They seemed to be loyal citizens all right, but who knew what was going on in their minds? And it was completely unpredictable what they would do if war put a real stress on the State. They had lived under Israeli rule for nineteen years and now seemed to have a good chance of embracing their brethren once again. Were they ready for the embrace? Were they eager? For years after the establishment of the state they had been treated like second-class citizens and were, obviously, suspect. They could not really resent this suspicion. Even today they were not called up for military service. But, quite apart from real or imaginary grievances, if the Israelis could not be blamed in the early fifties for treating the Arabs with a certain amount of suspicion, today the Arabs could not be blamed for rejoicing at the thought of living under Arab rule once again.

But they did not rejoice.

It would be untrue to say that they gave no trouble at all during the Six Day War. But it is perfectly true that they gave no serious trouble. For every display of hesitation, intrigue and contact with the enemy, there were a hundred manifestations of loyalty to Israel. Many Arabs offered sums of money – small or large, according to their financial position – to help the war effort; many donations were sent anonymously; thousands of Arabs went to the tax office to pay their taxes – not yet due

– in advance; many found other ways of expressing their loyalties and quite a few volunteered for military service. In the end, they were pleased that 'we have won'. Amazingly, this was the way they put it: *we:* Israelis and Israeli Arabs; *they*, the rest of the Arab world.

This may sound too good to be true. So it sounded to me at first. But the Israeli Arabs had several good reasons for fearing an Arab invasion. Many people in the Arab camps called the Israeli Arabs traitors who ought to suffer for their co-operation with Israel. The word 'massacre' was heard here and there and if it was certainly not official Arab policy, who could tell what individual soldiers would do in hours of martial excitement? Perhaps such fears were unfounded; perhaps they were much too pessimistic. But the vast majority of Israeli Arabs would not have been too happy to put this to the test. (Quite a few Arabs – outside Israel – regarded the coming day of Arab triumph as the day of general reckoning. Around Bethlehem there were whispers in Moslem circles – who are a minority there – about massacres of Christian Arabs. The whispered slogan was: 'We'll finish off the Saturday people first, then come the Sunday people.' The Sunday people were, of course, the Christian Arabs; the Arabs themselves were the Friday people.)

The first postwar encounters between Israeli Arabs and the Jordanian Arabs of the West Bank were not too happy. When the first Jordanians – formerly Palestinian Arabs – ventured over to Israel, they were surprised to find so many Arabs alive; and not only alive but obviously quite content, living in little houses of their own, holding good jobs, sending their children to well-run schools, often possessing such treasures as a washing-machine or even a motor-car and enjoying an altogether higher standard of living than they, the Jordanians did. They felt a little jealous, angry, envious. The best way to soothe these feelings was to whisper: the rewards of treason.

When, in turn, the Israeli Arabs went over to visit Jordan, they were shocked by their cousins' backwardness, poverty, ignorance and lack of freedom. 'But for the grace of Allah there go I' they thought and were slightly ashamed of their thoughts.

The grace of Allah, after all, was that they had lived under Israeli rule.

There is no denying that the Israeli Arabs felt a bit superior and looked down upon their Palestinian brethren with an air of condescension. A tiny matter but a characteristic one: I heard an Israeli Arab bus-conductor tell how a Jordanian Arab had asked him to stop the bus because he wanted to get off. (That's what they do in Jordan where there are no fixed stops.) The Israeli Arab went on with a great deal of self-satisfaction and with a paternalistic smile: 'I explained it to him that *we* didn't do things that way. . . .'

When many Arabs fled in 1948, the Arab masses remaining in Israel were left leaderless. Arab society is pretty feudal and the community leaders were invariably members of old and privileged families. Most of the Arab leaders left in 1948 and, for the first time in Palestinian Arab history, men of common origin rose to become leaders purely on merit. This fact caused further friction after the June war. The self-made Israeli leaders were proud of their position and achievement; the old, feudal types on the other side of the former frontier regarded them as *parvenus*.

The mayor of one Israeli Arab town went over to a small Jordanian town on the West Bank, near the Latrun salient, to visit its mayor. The Israeli mayor was a self-made man who had risen to his position thanks to the confidence of the townspeople; his host held *his* position as his birthright, was a member of the establishment and had, indeed, been nineteen years earlier the mayor of the town which the Israeli Arab had come from. The West Bank gentleman was the Israeli mayor's predecessor and had known him as a humble villager. Today he felt it an imposition that he was supposed to treat him as an equal. All the same, the Israeli Arab mayor was received with every outward sign of courtesy and hospitality and offered coffee and cold drinks; but conversation was somewhat halting. Then the Arab mayor told a parable: one of the ancient Arab parables all Arabs are so fond of.

'Once upon a time there was a dog,' he began, 'whose great dream in life was to become a wolf. He went to Father

Wolf and told him about his dream. He *looked* like a wolf, why could he not *be* a wolf? Father Wolf replied: "If you want to be a wolf and live among wolves you must do as wolves do." "Yes," agreed the dog, "will you teach me what to do?" "First of all," said Father Wolf, "when wolves meet they do not smell one another's behinds but one another's noses. That is the most important rule." The dog nodded, went away and lived with the wolves very happily for nineteen years. After all this time he met Father Wolf again. He greeted Father Wolf, went up to him and started smelling his nose. But Father Wolf told him: "Don't bother. I know you are a dog. You may smell my arse all right." '

An uncomfortable silence fell in the room when this parable ended. A few seconds later the Israeli Arab mayor rose, walked out of the room and banged the door behind him.

* * *

The West Bank Arabs – without noticing it themselves – are becoming half-Israeli Arabs. Of course, they have a long way to go and most of them wish to return to Jordanian rule. But some Arabs – outside Israeli occupied territories – start looking at *them* with suspicion. That is the way of Palestine. Every new situation arising after each war is entirely and utterly unacceptable to the Arabs; after each new defeat they start hankering after the *former* status quo which they had declared totally repugnant. The passage of time has turned many Palestinian Arabs into Israeli Arabs and will turn many West Bank Arabs into half-Israeli Arabs. And the United Nations will go on holding session after session.

* * *

The Bedouins – much more nomadic in 1948 than today – were always more pro-Israeli than the rest. In the old days they robbed many Israelis but there was nothing personal, let alone anti-Jewish, in that. They robbed people worth robbing.

Even in those days some of the Bedouin felt grateful for the medical treatment they had received in the *kibbutzim* and a handful of them fought on Israel's side even in 1948.

I saw a few hundred of them now settled in villages between Haifa and Nazareth, most respectable, law-abiding citizens. I went to the former chief's house and he received me with warm Arab hospitality. I had my romantic notions: poor Bedouins, sons of the vast and infinite desert, settled in brick houses in ordinary villages. How awful! But the Bedouins did not feel half as sorry for themselves as I felt for them; they were not such romantic souls as I was. This was a welcome change, the former chief said simply. It was much more comfortable – he added – to live in a house than to keep moving your tent from place to place. Better for the children too; they could attend school. It was very pleasant indeed to have a properly furnished house, a refrigerator, a television set and a tin-opener fixed to the wall.

'But what about the freedom of the desert?' I pressed him hopefully.

'Oh yes . . .' he said. 'The freedom of the desert. Well, this life has its compensations, you see.'

'No desire to roam the infinite waste-land, feeling absolutely free?' I asked.

'None whatsoever,' he replied.

An Arab friend, accompanying me, said: 'Not so long ago every drop of water had to be fetched by women.'

'Men could have helped,' I remarked.

'From time immemorial it has always been the duty of women to fetch water. But this is not my point. If, in those days, a guest asked for a glass of water, he would get it, of course, but this was a major disaster. Today they turn the tap on.'

'What about tribal feuds?' I asked hopefully.

'They are buried,' said the ex-chief. 'They do not survive in villages.'

'But there used to be deadly enmities,' I argued. 'Irreconcilable blood feuds.'

'All reconciled.'

He smiled: 'Our minds were small in those days.'

*   *   *

Near Beersheba the Bedouins have their own Duke of Bedford. He is as charming, likeable and resourceful as our own. For a hundred Israeli pounds you can have tea with this Bedouin chief, squatting on the floor, in his tent.

I am told he does not actually live in the tent. He only works there. After office hours he ceases to be a nomad and returns to his comfortable house in Beersheba (running hot water, WC and stereo-gramophone with loudspeakers in three rooms).

*   *   *

If any Zionist or pro-Zionist, talking to an Arab, suggests that Arabs in Israel are well-off and that this compensates for many things, the Arab will be indignant and I, for one, sympathize with his indignation. Economic well-being is not everything. Ask any man in the Gaza Strip if he would be prepared voluntarily to give up his freedom and live under Israeli rule even if he could then live like a prince; he would reject any such idea with anger and scorn. But the Israeli Arabs – who have actually tasted the benefits of a better life – think differently. It is like the freedom of the desert, all over again: *I* want it for the Bedouin but the Bedouin does not want it for himself. Perhaps if the Arabs fully trusted the liberating Arab armies and the motives of the Arab rulers they would think differently. I don't know. The Israeli Arabs are proud people, as fond of their freedom and as nationalistically minded as anyone. Yet, at the moment most of them seem to be perfectly content under Israel's yoke.

Apart from not being called up for military service (for wars in which they could not possibly face any enemy other than their fellow Arabs) they are equal citizens in a democratic country and, in fact, a large number of them are active in the Labour Party. (Many others support the Communist Party –

the pro-Soviet branch. They do this although they are anti-Communists; but the Communist Party – as I explained earlier – is the only pro-Arab Party for Arab nationalists to support.) The Israeli Arabs, on the whole, are well-off; they can fulfil many of their ambitions and bring their children up to a much better life than their cousins are able to do on the West Bank or in Jordan. Three thousand Arab men have married Jewish girls (although, as far as I could find out, not one single Jew has married an Arab girl). The Israeli Arabs work hard, trying to save up for houses, television sets, washing-machines and motor-cars. In other words, more often than not they turn away from politics and their main ambition in life is to keep up with the Levys.

* * *

All Israeli Arabs are not what they seem. I was travelling near Beersheba with a group of Israeli journalists in search of local colour. One of them was told to contact a Bedouin who was stationed near a small inn on the main road, and looked particularly picturesque. So picturesque, indeed, that his main job was being picturesque: tourists, mostly Americans, photographed him with his camel all day long for fees ranging from I£5 to I£10. He did a roaring trade.

We found the man without difficulty – in fact, it would have been impossible to miss him. He looked fierce; he looked magnificent; his skin was scorched by the desert sun; his eyes burnt a hole in your face when he stared at you. There was centuries of pride, wisdom, ferocity and courage in this man – yet he was quite approachable.

He talked to one of the Israeli journalists and I listened. They talked Hebrew but I still listened. An American tourist couple interrupted us – the woman wanted to be photographed with the Bedouin in front of the camel; they paid him I£10 (about £1.5.0 in English money) and left. The interview continued.

At last I interrupted them, in English.

'Your accent,' I said.

141

'What do you want with my accent?' he asked haughtily, a hundred desert suns burning in his black eyes.

'Your accent is not a Bedouin accent,' I told him.

'Perhaps it isn't.'

'Your accent is a Hungarian accent.'

'Perhaps it is.'

'What's your name?'

'Zoltan Steiner.'

'Zoltan Steiner,' I repeated, testing the name in my mouth. 'Let's face it: Zoltan Steiner is not a Bedouin name. At least not a common Bedouin name.'

'No. It's not a Bedouin name at all.'

'Then why are you dressed as a Bedouin?'

He looked at me, and only about fifty desert suns were burning in his eyes by now.

'It is my profession to be a Bedouin. Doctors dress for their jobs; surgeons and nurses do too; soldiers, policemen and miners dress for their jobs; and nuns and rabbis; why not Bedouins?'

He had a point.

'Come on, Mr Steiner. Tell me how does a Hungarian Jew become a professional Bedouin outside Beersheba?'

He told me. It was a straightforward story. He had been down and out in Beersheba, no job and not a penny to his name. He noticed that a Bedouin – a genuine son of the desert – was doing roaring business being photographed by American tourists. One day the tribe – still semi-nomadic – decided to move on. The Bedouin who earned his livelihood as a photographic model fought this decision tooth and nail: he was doing well. But the rest of the tribe was doing badly and what could one man do against all of them? It was unthinkable, of course, that he should stay put while the others left: no Bedouin would separate from the tribe. So he left with the others.

'On that day,' Mr Steiner continued, 'I went to Beersheba market and bought Bedouin garments. It was not cheap because I had to be pretty picturesque, but I got credit. I also bought a camel. On hire-purchase. But he's all paid up by now. At lunch time – on the very day the others left – I was already here. I have never looked back.'

He looked at his wristwatch.

'Are you in a hurry?' I asked.

'Not yet. I close at 5.30. At 7.30 in the season.'

'What do you do afterwards?'

'Go home, have a bath and well . . . one thing or another. Usually I listen to my stereo. Mozart is my favourite. I prefer early Mozart to late. I am an unusual man.'

I did not deny that.

'Are you happy and content, Mr Steiner?' I asked him.

He looked at me. By this time I saw that the dark gleam in his fierce eyes was the reflection of the lights in a hundred Central European cafés.

'Yes, I am happy and content,' he said quietly, 'except for one thing.'

'What is that?'

'I am still frightened to death of this bloody camel.'

Kibbutz Hilton

We drove into the kibbutz and went to Reception. We saw a few signs: DINERS CLUB CARDS ACCEPTED HERE and AMERICAN EXPRESS TRAVELERS CHEQUES WELCOME. We registered and our luggage was taken to our room by a page-like person. The room was complete with shower and air-conditioning. Later we went to the dining-room, full of American tourists, the same people we had seen in the Hilton at Tel-Aviv; the same people you can see in Hiltons all over the world. The only unusual phenomenon was that the Americans here had dressed down – polo-neck shirts, Bermuda shorts – because, after all, this was a *kibbutz*. The dining-room of the *kibbutz* itself – as distinct from the hotel dining-room – was far away and had nothing to do with this place. The *kibbutzniks* kept away and lived and ate like *kibbutzniks* everywhere.

'Only the barman, the receptionist and the manager of the restaurant are members of the *kibbutz*,' someone informed me. 'The waitresses are hired because the *kibbutzniks* refuse to serve other people.'

This was not true, as I learnt later. The manager of the restaurant, a member of the *kibbutz* who held the rank of colonel in the army, walked around at coffee-time, bowed to people (slightly) and said: 'I hope you've enjoyed your meal.'

I remembered the *kibbutzim* I had seen twenty years before: their struggle, their poverty, their simplicity, and I was pleased to see how prosperous they had become. One cannot help asking oneself at the same time: has anything been lost in the process? Today they all run industries – this one runs a hotel, others produce agricultural implements, machine

tools, electrical and other goods – and most of their members live a civilized and comfortable life. This place is perhaps richer than most and certainly much richer than the little English *kibbutz* a friend of mine had visited a few days before, where everyone has tea at four in the afternoon and plays cricket on Saturdays. A portrait of the Queen hangs on the wall. My friend asked one of the *kibbutzniks* if they were all English or did they have other nationalities among them? The English boy was surprised and shook his head: 'Oh no. No foreigners here.' My friend expected him to add: 'And no Jews either.'

Here, in Kibbutz Hilton, I made some remark about their affluence to the colonel, who smiled.

'I am so sorry we are not in rags. People resent this. We are supposed to be ragged pioneers and they are disappointed. We are considering whether to order our chaps on duty in the hotel to put on rags to please our guests.'

I told him that I did not mind the absence of rags so much – although rags were always picturesque – but I was surprised to hear that they had hired hands from outside because they found waiting on people infra dig.

'It's quite true that the use of hired labour is contrary to all *kibbutz* principles. It is also true that in spite of this we do hire girls from the neighbouring village who make good money here. But it is absolutely untrue that we do this because we find waiting on people infra dig. We would not ask other people to do work we refuse to do ourselves. But we simply don't have enough members to do all the work in the hotel section *and* run the *kibbutz*. After all the work of the *kibbutz* – agriculture, cotton-growing – comes first. The hotel is an important and profitable side-line, but only a side-line. One day, when we have built a lot of new houses, members will serve in the restaurants or perhaps the other way round: the outside waitresses – those who wish it anyway – will be accepted as members.'

The idea of mutual aid is still the dominant principle of *kibbutz* life. Able sons of members are sent to university; but when they come back they still have to do the ordinary jobs.

A university graduate may become secretary but will still have to take his turn at the washing-up or waiting on members in the ordinary dining-room of the *kibbutz*. A brilliant fighter pilot with an outstanding record in the Six Day War was peeling potatoes when I visited the kitchen; the idea that he was doing a job beneath his dignity had obviously not even entered his mind. A former president of the *kibbutz* was at work in the orchard and very happy he was to be rid of a position which carried a great deal of responsibility and kept him indoors. Some members become ministers in the government but remain members of the *kibbutz*. When they cease to be ministers, they return to the *kibbutz* to clean stables or milk cows. Such members, however, are invariably pointed out to tourists: 'Look, that's an ex-minister, milking the cows.'

I met a pleasant, cultured and modest – almost shy – member who spoke good English with a slight Central European accent – German, I thought, but it could have been Polish. He was a middle-aged man and had spent most of his adult life in this *kibbutz*. 'I come from Britain,' he said, 'I am a British subject. I went to school there and all my relations live there. Let's leave it at that.' I did not, of course, ask him any further questions about his origins; I felt that he had good reasons for trying to forget his Central European past. His name was Alex and he remained my constant companion for my stay. I asked him what the role of *kibbutzim* was today. Were they mostly military outposts? Strategic fortifications? He shook his head.

'No. They have their military significance. It is also true that the *kibbutzim* played an important part in the war. There are many pilots and tank-officers among us. But believe it or not, an agricultural settlement is still, first and foremost, an agricultural settlement.'

I asked him what had happened to this particular agricultural settlement during the war, so near the Syrian border, in fact within easy shelling range.

'We were very lucky. We had tons of green fodder piled up here and one of the first Syrian shells hit it. The fodder caught

fire and burnt like mad for a long time, sending up a huge column of black smoke for hours. The Syrians must have thought they had hit an ammunition dump and blown us all up. The smoke made observation impossible. So they stopped shelling and left us in peace.'

All this sounded very simple. I told him that I had heard many stories about the heroism of *kibbutzniks*.

'Heroism?' he frowned. 'I'm not sure if that's the right word. The truth is that we could not retreat. Retreat is simply one of the few luxuries even the new and prosperous *kibbutzim* cannot afford. The Russians won major wars by retreating tactics and their scorched earth policy; but Kutuzoff would be a very small general in Israel. One can give up "territory"; one cannot give up one's home; one cannot scorch the work of one's whole lifetime. Yes, our *kibbutz* is our life – it is as simple as that. If we have to give up our lives – very well, this means that we have to die defending the *kibbutz*. This is not heroism; this is common sense.'

He spoke of everything – war, peace, life, death – calmly and without rhetoric. I liked him and admired his character but I thought he was completely without emotion. I was wrong. There was one subject which touched deep emotions in his heart. As soon as that subject was broached, he waxed lyrical, emotional, excited; his eyes began to shine, his voice grew warm. This subject was spare parts.

First he mentioned it casually. I had asked him what his job was and he answered: 'I look after spare parts,' and went on talking of other things.

Later, in his neat little house, he showed me his absent son's paintings. Very good paintings for an amateur. I asked him if he himself had a hobby.

'My hobby is my job,' he answered simply.

'Spare parts?' I asked.

'Yes,' he nodded.

'That's your hobby? Spare parts?'

Agriculture in this *kibbutz* is as highly mechanized as on any American farm. Many US visitors admitted this with admiration. Alex had noticed years before that a lot of time was wasted after break-downs in getting spare parts, often from Britain, sometimes even from the United States. So he persuaded the *kibbutz* Committee to keep spare parts there, ready for all emergencies. Alex's plan involved a large investment, so the Committee was reluctant at first. But Alex was adamant and his enthusiasm infectious, so in the end the Committee agreed and put him in charge of the spare parts department. The plan proved an enormous success. Many other *kibbutzim* have copied it since. Thousands of man-hours are being saved per annum and today his spare parts are housed in a large, separate building.

'Would you like to see my spare parts?'

It was clearly impossible to refuse so I said yes, I would love to see his spare parts. We went to the building and spent well over an hour there, inspecting cog-wheels, nails, screws, dynamos of all sizes and shapes and also more elaborate machine parts. I recalled one or two Englishmen who had taken me through their vegetable gardens: they glowed with the same pride in their cauliflowers and marrows as Alex did in his cog-wheels and plugs. Nowhere else had I met the same touching pride, loving care and human devotion to *things* – completely free of conceit and snobbery. He loved his spare parts with unselfish devotion, for their own sake.

'I went abroad in 1960. The *kibbutz* gave me the money and paid for everything. I went to Birmingham to visit my relations.'

Then he added: 'They paid the round trip,' lest I should think he was given a single ticket only.

'Everybody travels. All the youngsters in the *kibbutz* get trips. I'll go again – I *think* I'll go – in 1970. I'm due then.'

'But listen, Alex,' I told him, 'if you were a *dealer* in spare parts, half as successful as you are with your spare parts as a *kibbutznik*, you could afford trips round the world every year, not miserable little journeys every ten years.'

'That's true,' he said, with the air of a man who had thought of it many times.

'Well – no regrets?'

He did not ask me 'no regrets for what?' He knew. He

remained silent but I prodded him: 'No regrets for having become a monk in Israel?'

'One day,' he said, 'our generator broke down. The fault was in a small part of a special transformer, US made. Before I started my spare parts department, such a break-down would have meant a full stoppage for all our electricity-driven machinery – and our lighting – for at least three weeks. As it was, with the spare parts in my store-room, the break-down lasted seventeen minutes.'

'Congratulations. But I asked you: no regrets?'

'That's the answer. No regrets. True, I have no personal possessions. Perhaps we *are* the monks of Israel. But are we so much worse off than townspeople? We have no money, but they have to pay for everything. We get all we need, free of charge. We have no worries; no financial worries, at least. And as you can see, our standard of living has improved enormously. We used to live in cells, worse than monks; but this house of mine is quite pleasant, quite middle-class. We dress like townspeople, we often wear ties – a garment unknown in Israel twenty years ago. The whole *kibbutz*-system is mellowing. Children can spend much more time with their parents than before. My son used to live with us – my wife is away at the moment – until he joined the army. Private radios were discouraged in the past: one was supposed to listen to the communal radio. Today we all have our private radio sets and soon, no doubt, we'll have our private television sets, too. We live normal lives, like normal people in the towns. More and more of our children go in for degrees – just like youngsters outside.'

'Do they come back afterwards?'

'Some don't, most of them do. They like this life – they've been used to it all their lives. We have our social life. Our clubs. Everything is free in our clubs: you ask for a sandwich or for soft drinks and get it. For alcoholic drinks we have to pay from our pocket-money but who drinks? You know, this is one of the grave crimes of the Jews: they don't drink. Perhaps a few beers, that's all.'

He lit a cigarette.

It was important for him that the *kibbutz*-community was 'normal'.

'In the old days it was unheard of to lock one's room or house. The theory was: there are no thieves among us. But in practice we did have thieves. Petty thieves, I admit, but a few things disappeared. So now we lock up.'

He said this with some satisfaction. He was proud of the thieves of the *kibbutz*. Perhaps armed robbery would have been better but one should appreciate what one's got. A few petty thieves made the *kibbutz* less virtuous and more human. Thieves were *normal*.

'I know you asked me whether I have any regrets. I've been thinking a lot about this but, by now, I am certain: no, I have no regrets. Perhaps I've missed some fun. But what is fun? The *kibbutz* is not a place for ambition – that is, not for personal ambition. The *kibbutz*, as a *kibbutz*, is very ambitious indeed; and as you can see, very successful. Ours is a saner society than the competitive consumer society outside. In the outer world your preoccupation is: what you can *get*; here: what you can give. Not a bad life, you know. It has its hardships, its sacrifices; but it also has its compensations.'

'I see,' said I, and I really did see.

'Doing a useful job well, helping to build something worth-while, even great, one can also fulfil one's ambitions.'

He said this simply and it all sounded true and convincing. Yet I still wondered if he was not protesting just a shade too much.

'I have been the part of a whole,' he said and looked at me with pride.

'Not only a part,' I told him, 'a spare part.'

He smiled faintly and looked prouder still.

Sabras

The word *sabra* has changed its meaning twice.

Originally it was the name of a small, prickly, sourish fruit; then it came to mean a youngster, a native of Israel. Twenty years ago a *sabra* was something of a rarity in that country of immigrants; today just over half of the people are actually natives of Israel. So the word has changed its meaning once again. The *sabra*, by tradition, should be independent, aggressive, non-sentimental – non-Jewish, indeed: prickly and sourish. Many *sabras* are: but so are many immigrants. On the other hand, the six or seven children, say of a Moroccan family, actually born in Israel but brought up in the old-fashioned, Oriental tradition, are as remote from the *sabra* as the Koran is from Moshe Dayan.

There are fewer people around today who would tell you with pride shining in their eyes that their children are *sabras*, than there were twenty years ago. The word has been devalued but the *sabra* spirit is needed more in Israel today than the self-mockery, wisdom, understanding, self-pity and self-derogatory humour of the ghetto-Jew – for whom the *sabra* feels contempt.

The *sabra* is a Jewish nationalist and often an anti-Zionist.

The *sabra* is not impressed by his so-called benefactors – the rich Jews of America and other countries of the diaspora – and is doubtful about their motives. When volunteers from all over the world were trying to come to Israel during the Six Day War, the *sabras* said: 'We don't want them. Besides, all they want is a free holiday.' Learning of the number of girls among them, they added: 'All they want is to catch a husband.'

When they heard that the Vatican had forgiven the Jews, or rather had exonerated them from responsibility for the crucifixion, they asked: 'And who will forgive the Popes and the Vatican for 2,000 years of persecution?'

They are rebellious against authority, but not militant. They took no pleasure in the Six Day War. The war and the defeat of those foolish Arabs was a distasteful duty, a sheer waste of time. It has to be done every now and then and they are ready for the next round, but without feeling any enthusiasm for the task. They perform this duty as the farmer performs the duty of weeding: it is hard and unpleasant work, but necessary.

There are violent student demonstrations all over the world but not in Israel. The tough, aggressive youth of Israel keeps away from demonstrations; they do not want 'student power' and feel no desire to reform society. Israel has no Cohn-Bendit or Tariq Ali. Israeli youth dislikes these people and they, in turn, hate Jewish nationalism. Israeli youth fails to see – or at least to appreciate – that many of these student leaders hate French, British and German nationalism, too, thus representing a broader and warmer vision of humanity than the narrow-minded nationalist. Perhaps they know all this but hold that internationalism is a luxury Israel cannot afford. In any case, there are two main reasons for the absence of student unrest in Israel. First, the price of a degree is high and its reward is higher still. A young man, studying for a degree is dependent on his parents who, as a rule, have to make a great sacrifice for his studies; a man with a degree can count on a good job, independence and social status. So the youth of Israel finds it important to concentrate on his studies first and to try to reform society – if reform it he must – after getting his degree. There is little romance in being a student. The second reason, however, is the more important. These young people are not anti-establishment. This does not mean that they are enthusiastic supporters of every aspect of government policy: but they support it in its essentials and they, too, want to defend Israel from the Arabs. What else can they do? As there is no *basic* disagreement, protest marches and revolutionary acts would be pointless. Consequently Israel's young people spend their

time studying. Their aggressive instincts and surplus energy can be worked off during military service and the perennial wars.

The *sabra* is also impatient with the Jews of the diaspora. If the man is a Jew, he should come to Israel; if he doesn't come to Israel, he is not a Jew. He has an Israelo-centric *weltanschauung* and he views the world through Israeli spectacles. He knows of course that it would be narrow-minded to believe that the world has one single problem only; so he concedes that it has two: the problem of Israel versus the Arabs, and the problem of the Jews of Israel versus the Jews of the diaspora.

* * *

There have always been splits between the generations, but in two countries of our modern world the two generations faced each other with more than usual hostility, lack of understanding and suspicion: Germany and Israel.

Modern German youth asked their parents: how could you do it? Modern Israeli youth asked *their* parents: how could you tolerate it?

There existed a seemingly unbridgeable gap in both countries. Germany is not our subject here; in Israel it was the Eichmann trial which helped to clear the air. Until then the *sabras* took the well-known, primitive, martial attitude: why didn't our fathers revolt, shoot back and die fighting? For them the Nazi period was not an era of suffering and martyrdom but an era of shame. The parents, at the same time, refused to discuss these matters. It had been enough to live through those times: one could never forget but one could – and ought to – remain silent. The Eichmann trial[1] brought back the tragedy in its full horror: it showed that the Jews were defenceless against armed bullies and the might of the state but, wherever the situation permitted resistance, however hopeless – as in the Warsaw Ghetto – they died fighting. They also learnt – and that made the greatest impression on them – that in those days the world

[1] For an interesting view see the reprint of Professor J. Zellermayer's lecture delivered at the Hadassah University Hospital.

stood by, watched the massacre of innocent millions and pleaded ignorance afterwards. Their own experience in June 1967 clinched it all. They suddenly realized that it *might happen again*. Even the survivors of the holocaust could be massacred. What could the young heroes of 1967 do where their fathers failed in the forties? They would have been massacred, too – bearing arms, it is true – and the world would again have looked on. They learned to accept the fact that the mass murder of the Nazi era was a Jewish tragedy and no Jewish shame.

The Eichmann trial also taught them that one could *speak* of the unspeakable; that discussion clears the air; that the victims and – alas – even their murderers were human. It was brought home to them that the Eichmann period was the shame of Germany and not the shame of Jewry. And – most important of all – the trial coupled with the war taught both generations, old and young, one great lesson: the old felt, after the war, that given the chance and given the weapons, they, too, could have been heroes; and the *sabras*, having seen the massing of vast Arab armies crying murder and revenge on their frontiers and the world shedding tears but doing nothing, realized that they, too, could be victims.

*   *   *

The wheel has come full circle. The *sabra* who lives in a state which is outstanding in agriculture and war, mediocre in the arts and literature and poor in commerce and banking, and is bothered with permanent foreign exchange troubles, is a new species, a different kind of animal from his European-born father.

An Israeli couple took their eleven-year-old *sabra* son on a tour of Europe. In Italy the boy asked: 'Are these people Jews?'

'No,' said his father, 'they are Christians.'

In France he asked again: 'Are *these* people Jews?'

'No, they are Christians.'

The boy asked the same question – and got the same answer

– in Holland, Denmark and Sweden. Then he exclaimed with genuine sympathy:

'What a horrible fate!... It must be awful for poor Christians, being scattered like that all over the world.'